Patterns of Order and Utopia

Dorothy F. Donnelly

St. Martin's Press
New York

PATTERNS OF ORDER AND UTOPIA
Copyright © 1998 by Dorothy F. Donnelly. All rights reserved. Printed in
the United States of America. No part of this book may be used or repro-
duced in any manner whatsoever without written permission except in
the case of brief quotations embodied in critical articles or reviews. For
information, address: St. Martin's Press, 175 Fifth Avenue, New York,
N.Y. 10010.

ISBN 0-312-16496-3

Library of Congress Cataloging-in-Publication Data

Donnelly, Dorothy F., 1937-
    Patterns of order and Utopia / Dorothy F. Donnelly.
        p.   cm.
    Includes bibliographical references and index.
    ISBN 0-312-16496-3
    1. Utopias—History.   2. Order (Philosophy)—History.   I. Title.
HX806.D66   1998
321' .07'09—dc21   98-3794
                                                                  CIP

Design by Orit Mardkha-Tenzer

First edition: November 1998
10 9 8 7 6 5 4 3 2 1

To my niece
Patricia Laverty-Maguire

Contents

Preface

S ome of the material in this study was originally presented in scholarly books and journals (cited at the beginning of the appropriate chapter's notes) and is reprinted here with permission. This previously published material has been considerably revised and reflects the most recent critical commentary by those contemporary scholars currently participating in the dialogue on this book's subject. Throughout the text I have used the major translations of original sources. In an effort to make the work more generally accessible, I have in some cases modernized the spelling and occasionally used alternate words to conform to modern usage. Any changes in language are noted in brackets within the quotations taken from original sources.

Acknowledgments

*I*t is a pleasure to thank those individuals and institutions who have helped me in the preparation of this book. I am especially grateful to Michael J. Flamini, senior editor, Scholarly and Reference Division, St. Martin's Press, for his encouragement in planning this project and his important suggestions about possible directions for the book. I also want to acknowledge my indebtedness to Elizabeth Paukstis, editorial assistant, Ruth Mannes, production editor, and Wendy Kraus, associate production editor at St. Martin's Press, for their work in guiding the book through the production process with great patience and skill.

I would like to express my deep gratitude to Ethel Thompson for her invaluable assistance and outstanding work on this book, and without whom it could not have been completed. I also owe special thanks to Renee Somers, my research assistant, for her research contribution and general assistance in the preparation of the manuscript. I am indebted to Professor Victor Harris, formerly of Brandeis University, who early on encouraged and advised me in the pursuit of my scholarly interests and whose expertise helped draw out the implications of my research. For their help and support, I want to thank the library staffs at Brandeis, Brown, and the University of Rhode Island. Most of the research for this project was conducted at or through these libraries. I particularly want to express my appreciation to Jean Sheridan of the reference department at the URI library on the main campus who was extremely helpful in conducting comprehensive computer searches. Joanna Burkhardt, director of the library, was unfailing in her support of my work on this extended project. For their considerable help in locating and securing faraway resources relevant to this book, I also want to thank library staff members Marilyn Jamgochian, Cathy Poirer, and Lucinda Ugorji, and their student assistants Michelle Altrui, Naima A'vant, Tom Rich, and Phyllis Stanzler. Over the years, colleagues at Brandeis University, Brown, Villanova, and especially the University of Rhode Island have shared ideas and supported my endeavors. I thank them.

Finally, I would like to acknowledge that the publication of this book was assisted by a research grant from the University of Rhode Island Foundation Faculty Award Program, a grant from the Dean's Office, College of Arts and Sciences, University of Rhode Island, and assistance from the Office of the Provost.

On a more personal level, I am grateful to those many friends whose personal support has sustained me over the years. My most personal thanks and gratitude I owe to my niece, Patricia Laverty-Maguire, who consistently encourages and supports me with warmth and affection.

Dorothy F. Donnelly

Introduction

This book focuses on the close relation between the notion of order and classical utopianism. Most analysts of utopias and utopian thought have taken for granted that the defining characteristic of classical utopias is that they offer a description of an ideal commonwealth. Few scholars, however, have given serious attention to an essential feature of classical utopias—the place of order in the tradition of classical utopian thought. For the classical utopians, a central preoccupation in their utopian conceptualization is the explication of a new definition of order. I intend to discuss the radical role that a classical utopian writer's unique ordering vision has upon the particular kind of transforming ideal that is envisioned. I address this subject, first, via a summary discussion of the relevant thought of Plato and Aristotle, and then through a more detailed analysis of Augustine's *De Civitate Dei,* important political writings of Thomas Aquinas, Dante's *De Monarchia,* Marsilius of Padua's *Defensor Pacis,* Thomas More's *Utopia,* and Francis Bacon's *New Atlantis.*

The analysis of utopianism is complicated by the fact that there exists such a broad range of interpretations of the meaning of utopia. Several studies have discussed the similarities and differences among utopias, while others have compared utopia with otherworldly notions of an ideal existence for the purpose of arriving at a synthesis. On the one hand we have attempts to demonstrate that even though utopias have a common base they can nonetheless be divided into a number of different categories, and on the other it is suggested that *utopia* is an all-inclusive term and that such diverse works as religious writings, the myth of the Golden Age, and various millenarianisms are properly included under the rubric of utopia. As traditionally used the term *utopia* refers to works that present a descriptive picture of an ideal state or commonwealth. Contemporary usage finds it applied to any work containing elements of what is called utopian thought; that is, any social, intellectual, political, religious, or psychological theory that speculates about the possibilities of achieving the good life in the future. The tendency to draw distinctions among utopias and to divide them into opposite types gives us a great number of categories—the soft and the hard utopias, static and dynamic utopias, utopias of escape and utopias of reconstruction, ideal utopias and practical utopias, evolutionary, scientific, and arcadian utopias, prophetic and secular utopias. The search for synthesis has resulted in classifying as utopian such distinctly different kinds of expressions as religious writings (Old and New Testaments), political and social tracts outlining plans for restructuring social arrangements (Karl Marx's *Communist Manifesto* and M. J. A. N. Condorcet's *Sketch for the Historical Picture of the Progress of the Human Mind),* writings that set forth a plan for the redesigning of cities (Antonio Averlino's *Treatise on Architecture* and Leonardo Bruni's *Laudatio Florentinae Urbis),* and fictional works that present a picture of an ideal commonwealth (Thomas More's *Utopia* and Francis Bacon's *New Atlantis).*[1]

This ambiguity in definition and classification concerning utopia runs through the literature and is found in many works on utopia and the utopian mode of thought. I shall not attempt to review this extensive bibliography here, but it is necessary to consider briefly some of the more important inquiries into the subject so that the approach I shall present in this book will be more sharply focused. Two earlier studies on utopian literature which establish both the method of assigning utopias to specific categories and of making the term itself an all-inclusive one are Lewis Mumford's *The Story of Utopias* and Joyce O. Hertzler's *The History of Utopian Thought.* Mumford classifies utopias as either "utopias of escape" or "utopias of reconstruction" and places works such as Augustine's *The City of God,* William Morris's *News From Nowhere,* and H. G. Wells's *A Modern Utopia* in the former category and Plato's *Republic,* Thomas More's *Utopia,* and Tommaso Campanella's *City of the Sun* in the latter. Mumford's categories are based upon what he finds to be two opposing functions: "One of these functions is escape or compensation; it seeks an immediate release from the difficulties or frustrations of our lot. The other attempts to provide a condition for our release in the future. . . . The first leaves the external world the way it is; the second seeks to change it so that one may have intercourse with it on one's own terms."[2] Hertzler also believes that we need to use a broad approach in the search for utopian conceptualizations and therefore argues that any "conception of social improvement either by ideas and ideals themselves or embodied in definite agencies of social change" is a utopian work. This point of view leads Hertzler to the conclusion that the utopian tradition has its roots in the prophetic tradition, namely, in the "numerous utopian expressions" of the "Hebrew prophets."[3] This merging of "secular" and "prophetic" utopias is but one of several attempts at synthesis. Other approaches are seen in the claims that there exists a relationship between utopia and the myth of the Golden Age, the Garden of Eden, the pastoral tradition, and the Arcadia of the Renaissance. S. B. Liljegren, for example, in *Studies on the Origin and Early Tradition of English Utopian Fiction,* takes the position that English utopias have their origin in the "traditions of Eden in the Bible, of the Elysian Field of Homer, of the Insulae Fortunatae or the Island(s) of the Blessed of Greek and Latin authors, [and] of Plato's Atlantis,"[4] all of which intermingle with each other and with utopias as later envisioned by English authors of the fifteenth and sixteenth centuries. And Robert C. Elliott, who traces the roots of the utopian tradition back to the myth of the Golden Age, finds that the breakdown of the belief in the historical reality of the Golden Age led philosophers to transfer "the notion of an ideal life in the irrecoverable past into utopian tales of what the world might—even should—be like; the myth, that is, provided sustenance for a conceivable reality."[5] The idea that Liljegren proposes is that utopias have in common certain "ideal" qualities; and what Elliott argues, in effect, is that "utopia is the secularization of the myth of the Golden Age."

A more ambitious study on the conceptual level is Karl Mannheim's *Ideology and Utopia.* In his work Mannheim develops a theory of history as progressive and in this context analyzes the historical function of utopian thought. He proposes that all political thought can be divided into two classes, the ideological and the utopian. The mode of thought of those whose ideas resist social change he calls ideological and the outlook of those whose ideas work toward social change he names utopian.[6] Mannheim's theory is based on a view of society as a struggle between the desires of one group standing in opposition to those of another group. Paul Tillich, in his paper "Critique and Justification of Utopia," says that there exists an organic relationship between utopia and religion: "Judaism is perhaps the most momentous utopian movement in history, for directly or indirectly it has elevated all humankind to another sphere of existence through its utopia based on the coming Kingdom of God."[7] Tillich places utopia in a theological context and bases his ideas on the fundamental premise that utopia is rooted in human nature itself. His critique of utopia is developed from an analysis of what he describes as the positive characteristics of utopia—truth, fruitfulness, power—and utopia's negative characteristics—untruth, unfruitfulness, and impotence. His justification of utopia stems from his view that these opposing forces are resolved by what he defines as the transcendence of utopia. For Tillich, the fruitfulness of utopia is its "ability to open up possibilities"; its value is that in this tension between the impossible and the possible we find the means by which "life transcends itself."

A much different approach is taken by Frank Manuel in "Toward a Psychological History of Utopias." Writing as a philosophical and psychological historian, Manuel argues that in defining utopia the boundaries need not be narrowly drawn and his attitude, as he describes it, is "latitudinarian and ecumenical." He therefore classes as utopian any work that evokes "a vision of life . . . in an earthly paradise that would be radically different from the existing order." Under this rubric Manuel includes not only works in the classical utopian tradition (Thomas More, Tommaso Campanella), but also modern philosophical psychologists (Erich Fromm, Wilheim Reich, Abraham Maslow) and philosophers of history (Norman O. Brown, Herbert Marcuse). Manuel's approach is to study utopias as psychological documents that tell us about the sensibility of the societies in which they were produced. He thus distinguishes among three groups of utopias: "utopias of calm felicity," characteristic of the period from More's *Utopia* until the French Revolution; the "dynamic socialist and other historically determinist utopias" of the nineteenth century; and the "psychological and philosophical utopias" of the twentieth century, the "eupsychia."

4

In the first group the good life derives from a "wise order" of social arrangements. In the second, it is based on a "dynamic historical process" that emphasizes individualism and self-expression. And in the third (developed in reaction to the "denial of utopia by Darwin and Freud"), the vision of the good life emerges from the ideas of the life-scientists "who assert that a benign spirituality" is about to possess the whole of humankind and the philosophers of history who adapt the ideas of Darwin and Freud to "serve a utopian ideal."[8] Northrup Frye, in "Varieties of Literary Utopias," also thinks that "some of the most uninhibited utopian thinking today comes from such Freudians as Norman O. Brown (*Life Against Death*) and Herbert Marcuse (*Eros and Civilization*)." Frye defines utopia as a "speculative myth; it is designed to contain or provide a vision for one's social ideas, not to be a theory connecting social facts." The utopian writer, he suggests, "looks at the ritual habits of society and tries to see what society would be like if these ritual habits were made more consistent and more inclusive." In discussing the utopian mode of thought Frye, like Elliott and Liljegren, traces the "ideal" quality of utopia to the myths of the Golden Age and Paradise. Unlike these writers, however, Frye's purpose is to suggest a relationship between the myths of the Golden Age and Paradise and the pastoral tradition, the Arcadia of the Renaissance, and later utopias. He finds, for example, that the "eighteenth-century descendant of the pastoral myth was the conception of the 'natural society' in Bolingbroke, and later in Rousseau."[9]

Mention should also be made of Ernest Tuveson's important book, *Millennium and Utopia: A Study in the Background of the Idea of Progress.* Tuveson's study deals with the reappearance in the seventeenth century of a belief in a millennial end to history and the close relation between this belief and the idea of progress. As Tuveson states: "The millennium itself came to be considered as a true utopia. . . . The method of God . . . is one of progress by fixed stages of cultural development which result from the refinement of spiritual and mental faculties: the advance from the 'primitive' to the 'philosophical' stages is the story of human redemption."[10] In this secularization of the millennial theory, according to Tuveson, we find a new definition of salvation in which "evolution" and "stages of advancement" replace the theological doctrine of "grace."

Finally, in their comprehensive study of the history of utopian thought, *Utopian Thought in the Western World,* Frank Manuel and Fritzie Manuel find "the existence of a utopian propensity" that has manifested itself throughout Western society. Proposing that utopias must be analyzed on many different levels, they reject rigid definitions and dictionary labels. In a word, for the Manuels utopia has plural meanings. As they put it, "any strict compartmentalization of future utopias and nostalgia for an idealized bygone human condition is invalidated by their constant interplay in Western thought."[11] The Manuels' aim "is to endow the idea of utopia with historical meaning," and to demonstrate the claim of a persistent utopian impulse. Toward this end, they use a fluid rather than restrictive definition of the term *utopia.* In more recent studies, Timothy Kenyon and Krishan Kumar have taken other approaches to the subject of utopianism. Kuman, like the Manuels, identifies several kinds of ideal societies, of which utopia is only one. The five types of ideal societies or ideal conditions of humanity that Kumar identifies include: the Golden Age, Arcadia, Paradise, the millennium, and the ideal commonwealth. Kumar notes that "ideal-society types clearly overlap one another. Paradise is fused with the Golden Age; Cockaygne is a reproach to Arcadia while it borrows heavily from the Golden Age and Paradise; the millennium is Paradise restored; the ideal city draws upon the myths of ancient Golden Age civilizations."[12] Unlike the Manuels, however, he regards utopia as distinctly different from other notions of an ideal society because "utopia challenges by supplying alternatives. It shows what could be. But its most persistent function, the real source of its subversiveness, is as a critical commentary on the arrangements of society. Utopia, that is, is a form of social theory, and just as all social theory since the Greeks has always tried to do, utopia too gives an account of the contemporary predicament and suggests ways out of it."[13] Kenyon also offers a conceptual analysis of the subject of utopia and an overview of the intellectual background. Focusing on Thomas More's *Utopia* and the writings of Gerrard Winstanley, Kenyon approaches utopianism as a body of thought that is aligned with the history of political philosophy and political discourse. In response to the charge that utopias are a form of escapism or exercises in wishful thinking, Kenyon argues that "those utopias produced by thinkers such as More and Winstanley are far closer to what may be regarded as the mainstream of political thought than is often supposed."[14]

This review of the critical study on the subject suggests the variety of approaches taken in defining utopia. We see that often it is used in clearly contradictory ways: on the one hand it is applied to works which speak of a *telos* outside of time—an ideal supernatural existence; and on the other to an historical *telos*—an ideal human society. In the tendency to focus on similarities—in this instance on the fact of the conceptualization of the "good life"—commentators frequently ignore basic and, it might be argued, irreconcilable differences. For regardless of what form utopias take, or however much they differ in underlying assumptions and working principles, they have in common several basic propositions: they deal with ideas about the possibility of transforming and improving life in this world; they are not founded on supernatural truths; and they are not brought about by revelation or by divine intervention.[15] Thus even though the religious millennium and the Chiliastic Kingdom of God are to be established on this earth they are also in conflict with utopian thought since they too are brought about by divine intervention. Few would agree with the extreme restrictions imposed by Bertrand de Jouvenel when he suggests that "the designation of 'Utopia' should be denied to any exposition of a 'New Model' of Society which is bereft of pictures concerning daily life."[16] On the other hand, the persistent attempt to discern similarities between such different modes of thought as utopia and millennial themes often means that useful parameters are blurred. Clearly, a clarification of terms is necessary. The approach used in this study will be discussed below.

Let us turn now to the concept of order. The idea that order is an essential of reality has persisted as a dominant mode of thought throughout Western history. And a main characteristic of this tradition, from the time of the Greek period, has been the view that order in the temporal realm is inextricably linked with, and indeed dependent upon, extra-natural order.[17] There is, in other words, a belief that reality consists of an otherworldly realm of order and a this-worldly realm of order. In Greek thought there was a preoccupation with the attempt to establish a relationship between the order and constancy of the cosmos and the flux and change of the world of the senses. Indeed it is Plato's doctrine of two realms of order that is, in the opinion of many scholars, the primary source of the persistent mode of thought which views reality in terms of an otherworldly and a this-worldly scheme of order. Arthur O. Lovejoy, for example, puts it this way: "Plato . . . is the main historic source of the indigenous strain of otherworldliness in Occidental philosophy and religion, as distinguished from the imported Oriental varieties. . . . It is through him that the conception of an unseen eternal world, of which the visible world is but a pale copy, gains a permanent foothold in the West."[18]

A corollary feature of the historical attitude toward order is the view that cosmological order takes precedence over temporal order. Although they may approach the idea in different ways, Greek thinkers like Plato and Aristotle, for example, still share the same cosmological conclusion, namely, that while the phenomenal world is characterized by impermanence, overarching the world of change there is a single immutable order that is abiding and eternal—an order that is sustained by a top god that causes movement and life and sovereignly influences realms of order throughout the universe.[19] As Ernan McMullin has observed, Plato's view of cosmic harmony is that the manifold is to be understood as deriving from a transcendent sustaining principle of order.[20] The idea of attributing divine sanction to the concept of order characterizes its history prior to the Greek period. In the thought of the ancient Near East, among the peoples of Egypt and Mesopotamia, for instance, order was comprehended as of divine origin and as immanent in nature.[21] In Egyptian cosmology, order is the product of a creator-God who fashioned cosmic order out of formless chaos; and, this created principle of order permeates the entire physical world: "Ptah is throughout every body, . . . of all gods, of all [people], of all animals, of all creeping things, and of whatever lives."[22] Among the Mesopotamians too the cosmos was perceived as directed and controlled by divine order. However, contrary to the idea of a creator-God who imposed a given order, for the Mesopotamian "cosmic order did not appear as something given; rather it became something achieved—achieved through a continual integration of the many individual cosmic wills."[23] In brief, the fundamental assumption of both the Egyptian and Mesopotamian manner of viewing the world was the idea that order is of divine origin, that it governs the universe, and that it is embedded in nature.

Similarly, a dominant idea in the Hebraic-Christian tradition is the view that order takes precedence over disorder, and, further, that the order of the universe is divinely shaped. In the beginning, we are told in Genesis, "the earth was without form, and void; and darkness was upon the face of the deep" (Gen 1.2) and that it was the principle of order, in the form of God, who separated light from darkness, day from night, water from land, and who appointed the habitation of the sea to the fish, earth to the serpents and four-footed animals, sky to birds, and over all placed human beings—"over the fish of the sea, and over the fowl of the air, and over the cattle, and over all the earth" (Gen 1.26). In the Hebraic and Christian visions of order too temporal order is divinely ordained and cosmological order transcends all other order or orders.[24] It is thus not surprising that we find a preoccupation with the notion of order in the works of such writers as Augustine and Aquinas. "The peace of all things," says Augustine, "is the tranquillity of order. Order is the distribution which allots things equal and unequal, each to its own place."[25] And for Aquinas, "Divine Providence imposes order on all things, and thus the Apostle says truly (Rom. xiii.1) that 'the things which are of God are well ordered.'"[26] In Aquinas's view, "to take order away from creatures is to deny them the best thing that they have, because, though each one is good in itself, together they are very good because of the order of the universe."[27] And for both Augustine and Aquinas, the order appointed by divine providence includes all things. As Augustine says, "nothing can exist outside order"; and in Aquinas's words, "all things that exist are seen to be ordered to each other." Yet, at the same time, as we shall see in chapters 1 and 2, the systems of order developed by Aquinas and Augustine differ in very important ways. Whereas Augustine's notion of order is characterized by contrast and dichotomy, an order issuing in two different universal societies, on the one hand, and in a supreme ideal other world that inherently rejects this world on the other, for Aquinas order consists of two hierarchically different yet complementary orders, the natural order and the supernatural order.

Although there are significant differences in the way later thinkers developed their theories of order, they nonetheless share the fundamental assumption that order consists of an "otherworldly" realm of order and a "this-worldly" realm of order. This idea that order consists of both supertemporal and temporal realms was the regnant pattern of thought from the time of Augustine through the Middle Ages. During this long span there probably were some thinkers who questioned doctrine and/or practice; there were many too who were skeptical about the details of how divine order manifests itself; and there were even some, like St. Thomas Aquinas, Roger Bacon, St. Bonaventure, Dante, and Marsilius of Padua, who, greatly influenced by the Aristotelian revival of the thirteenth century, provided new ideas about the concept of order and about the nature of human nature. These thinkers, however, did not challenge the core idea that the order of the universe was in critical ways ultimately theocentric. Even in the fifteenth and sixteenth centuries when human reason had, in different places and in various areas of speculation, strongly reasserted its independence of the concept of religious order, the underlying assumption remained, for many thinkers, that the order of the universe is, finally, divinely ordained. Thus whatever other subjects they may treat, and however much their views may differ from traditional interpretations, we find that for most major writers, like Shakespeare and Spenser, for example, the order of the universe is still viewed as at once cosmic and composed of degrees or hierarchies that are interconnected. For Shakespeare's Ulysses

> The heavens themselves, the planets, and this centre
> Observe degree, priority, and place,
> Insisture, course, proportion, season, form,
> Office, and custom, in all line of order;
> And therefore is the glorious planet Sol
> In noble eminence enthron'd and spher'd
> Amidst the other. (*Troilus and Cressida,* Act 1, Scene iii)

Similarly, in Spenser's view

> He then them took, and tempering goodly well
> Their contrary dislikes with loved means,
> Did place them all in order, and compel
> To keep themselves within their sundry reigns,
> Together linkt with adamantine chains;

Yet so, as that in every living wight
The mix themselves, and show their kindly might.

So ever since they firmly have remained
And duly well observed his behest;
Through which now all these things are contained
Within this goodly cope, both most and least
Their being have. ("Hymn of Love")

In these passages there is represented the picture of a world pre-vented by a superior unifying order from falling into disorder or chaos. Above all cosmic or earthly order there is an order in general: "He then them took, and tempering goodly well/ Their contrary dislikes with loved means,/ Did place them all in order." Order is the first condition of everything that exists, and any rupture in "Heaven's first law" re-sults in the antithesis of order, cosmic anarchy: "Take but degree away, untune that string,/ And hark, what discord follows" (*Troilus and Cressida,* Act 1, Scene iii). The concept of order described in these lines is an ideal order which animates earthly order; the cosmic order is con-stituted of a hierarchical order of "degrees" put in place and main-tained—"So ever since they firmly have remained/ And duly well observed his behest"—in an harmonious whole. Each phenomenon in the world has its place, its "degree," in a divinely ordered universe.[28]

In a recent essay on order and disorder, Rudolf Arnheim notes that a pervasive striving for order seems to be inherent in the human mind. Arnheim claims that our "striving for order . . . derives from a similar universal tendency throughout the organic world; it is also paralleled by, and perhaps derived from, the striving towards the state of sim-plest structure in physical systems."[29] And Paul Kuntz argues that "hierarchy and the other modes of order are necessary because we find such structures in the cosmos, . . . and we create things following various principles of order. Hierarchy is necessary in thought because all the categories of being indicate how things are ordered and demon-strate degrees in all the dimensions."[30] It is thus not surprising to find a preoccupation with order also in the works of a wide range of mod-ern writers. According to Simone Weil, for example, "the first of the soul's needs, the one which touches most nearly its eternal destiny, is order." In Anais Nin the quest for order, as expressed in her *Diary* and her novelettes, takes the form of a search for harmony and unity among the fragmented parts of the self. And the search for order is a recurrent theme in the poetry of Wallace Stevens. For Stevens, even though the traditional concepts of order are no longer acceptable, nonetheless, it "is possible, must be possible," to satisfy our "blessed rage for order" and find meaningfulness in our world.

Keith Booker suggests that "utopian visions are in a fundamental sense literary in character; they have most commonly arisen within the realm of literature, and they are informed by fictionalized visions that empower alternative modes of thought."[31] While it is true that utopianism and literature are closely aligned, it is a mistake, I think, to view utopianism as discipline-bound. A broad multidisciplinary approach is required in the study of utopianism. One needs to resist the temptation, as Ruth Levitas reminds us, to "try to limit the field [of utopia studies] to one's own area of interest and set up boundaries which exclude large areas of material as not properly utopian."[32] In her recent comprehensive and insightful study of utopian thought, *The Concept of Utopia,* Levitas finds that utopianism has historically been studied from essentially three different perspectives: content, form, and function. According to Levitas, approaches to utopianism that privilege form, content, or function are, to a greater or lesser degree, problematic and fundamentally flawed precisely because they are unnecessarily restrictive. Levitas argues that the privileging of content is questionable because "definitions in terms of content tend to be evaluative and normative, specifying what the good society would be, rather than reflecting on how it may be differently perceived."[33] The privileging of form is problematic because it most often assumes that "utopia is a literary genre," on the one hand, and on the other that it "involves the fictional depiction of an alternative society in some detail."[34] And, the approach that privileges function needs to be viewed cautiously because using function as a defining characteristic fails to take into account the fact that "function is differently represented by different authors."[35] Instead of relying on strict definitions focused on function, form, or content, Levitas correctly argues for a definition of utopia that allows form, function, and content to vary markedly and to change over time. In contrast to narrow and restrictive definitions,

Levitas offers a new definition of utopia that is broad-ranging, inclusive, and which recognizes a common factor. For Levitas utopia is "the expression of the desire for a better way of being."[36]

In this study, I explore the integral relation between the idea of order and the classical utopia, and the emphasis is on the proposition that the expression of the desire for a better way of being in the classical utopia centered, first and foremost, on redefining order. While the study will of necessity consider such other matters as the connection between grace and reason, nature and natural law, and the individual and the state, its main focus is on an analysis of the influence of the notion of order on the general character of a tradition—the classical utopia from Plato's *Republic* to Francis Bacon's *New Atlantis*. I approach the works studied here with the conviction that if there is any universal aspect or common ground in classical utopias it is that each subsequent utopian vision presents a radically different view of order which, at the moment it is proposed, attempts in fundamental ways to invalidate the order that was previously perceived. We shall see, not surprisingly, that the demise of the classical utopia coincides with the decline in the view that order is fixed, stable, and unchanging.

The first chapter of this book examines the relationship between Plato's *Republic* and Augustine's *The City of God* and the connection, if any, between Augustine's work and the classical utopian mode of thought. The chapter points out that while some critics, as we have already seen, cite *The City of God* as an example of a utopian work, utopia and *The City of God* are based upon significantly different underlying assumptions and premises. Specifically, for our purposes, we find that the different concepts of order expressed in the *Republic* and *The City of God* result in works that inherently oppose each other in their ideas concerning the nature of the good life. The chapter concludes with the argument that not only is *The City of God* not an example of utopian writing, but that it may even be regarded as both a rejection of the utopian mode of thought and an injunction against utopian speculation.

Chapter 2 begins with a discussion of how Thomas Aquinas's ideas about a universal scheme of order directly challenged the Augustinian point of view. Influenced not by the ideas of Plato but by the revival in the twelfth century of the writings of Aristotle, the contrast and dichotomy of Augustine's dual system of order gives way in Aquinas to a concept of two orders that are different yet complementary. And these orders are not opposite orders in conflict; rather they are orders which support and supplement each other. The next chapter examines Dante's *De Monarchia* and Marsilius of Padua's *Defensor Pacis* as important utopian writings that significantly contributed to the redefinition in the Middle Ages of the concept of order. In brief, I propose that the utopianism we find in Aquinas, Dante, and Marsilius is directly linked to their views about order.

Chapter 4 of the book offers a discussion of the profound influence Duns Scotus's ideas about the relationship between faith and reason and, more specifically, his challenging argument that truth is twofold, had on contemporary definitions of order. The chapter examines how Thomas More incorporated the ideas of Aquinas, Dante, Marsilius, and Duns Scotus in the *Utopia,* and the several ways More went beyond these earlier thinkers in his treatment of the connection between universal and temporal order. The chapter concludes with a discussion of the claim that More's ordering vision inevitably gave rise to Francis Bacon's proposal that all order is characterized by change, not by stability. Chapter 5 argues that in the thought of Francis Bacon we find those ideas and that perspective which served as the impetus for dissolving classical as well as medieval concepts of order and, thus, at the same time, ended the tradition of the classical utopia. The chapter points out that whereas Thomas More proposed in *Utopia* that the good life might be achieved through a fixed and smoothly functioning structure of political order, Francis Bacon proposes in his *New Atlantis* that the good life could only be accomplished by means of an ordering system that is at once dynamic and progressive. The chapter concludes that Bacon's views mark a critical stage in the ultimate demise of classical utopianism precisely because it brings to an end all of the old ways of perceiving order.

In a final chapter, I summarize, from a slightly different perspective, my argument that an ever-changing attitude toward order played a major role in the history of classical utopian thinking and I suggest that this change in perspective resulted in, among other things, the modern shift from utopia to dystopia with its emphasis not on envisioning a "new world" but, rather, on a critique of the flaws in the societies on which they focus. Other commentators on utopianism have proposed that the disappearance of the classical utopia resulted from the influence of the ideas of Marx and Engels. Still others have argued that the decline resulted from the new emphasis on scientific inquiry in all areas of human thought. Judith Shklar, for instance, suggests that "the classical utopia lost its intellectual function with the rise of scientific socialism, especially Social Darwinism.[37] In contrast to these views, it is the argument of this book that the demise of classical utopianism is directly linked to the change in attitude toward the notion of order.

Chapter 1

Paradise vs. Utopia:
Augustine's *The City of God*

*I*n the *Retractations* Augustine explains that in writing *The City of God* he had a twofold purpose in mind. The work was intended not only to refute the "worshipers of many false gods, whom we call by the customary name pagans, attempting to attribute [Rome's] destruction to the Christian religion," but also to articulate a positive theological doctrine: "But lest anyone charge that we have only argued against the beliefs of others, and have not stated our own, it is just this that the second part of this work . . . accomplishes."[1] Thus whereas the primary purpose of classical utopian writers is to discuss ideas about political and social arrangements along secular lines and within the context of a concept of order that focuses, ultimately, on the relationship between the individual and the state, Augustine says forthrightly that his intention in *The City of God* is to present a descriptive analysis of the *operati Dei* and that his method is to do this within the context of an inquiry into the "origin, course, and final merited ends of the two cities, by which I mean the earthly and the heavenly."[2] In the development of his argument Augustine takes care that his particular use of the term "city" remains foremost by reiterating many times and in a number of ways the distinction he makes between the earthly city and the City of God. For example, he says in chapter 1 of book 14:

> And thus, in consequence, notwithstanding the many great nations that live throughout the world . . . nevertheless there

have arisen no more than two classes, as it were, of human society. Following our Scriptures, we may speak of them as two cities. For there is one city of [persons] who choose to live carnally, and another of those who choose to live spiritually.[3]

In chapter 1 of book 15 it is put this way:

I distinguish two branches of [humankind]: one made up of those who live according to [human nature], the other of those who live according to God. I speak of these branches also allegorically as two cities, that is, two societies of human beings of which one is predestined to reign eternally with God and the other to undergo eternal punishment with the devil.[4]

Augustine stresses that *civitas* is not synonymous with *res publica* or the state. On the contrary, the distinction is consistently between two universal societies: the society of the *civitas terrena* and the society of the *civitas Dei*. Whatever the opposing terms may be—City of God and city of human beings; heavenly city and earthly city; love of God and love of this world; love of the spirit and love of the flesh; the soul and the body—they always refer to members of a society, or *civitas,* who are distinguished not by social or political arrangements nor by allegiance to any earthly polity but, rather, by the commitment of their love: "The two cities then were created by two kinds of love: the earthly city by a love of self carried even to the point of contempt of God, the heavenly city by a love of God carried even to the point of contempt for self."[5] Any critique of Augustine's *The City of God* must be based on an understanding of his figurative use of the term *city.* As we see, in Augustine *civitas terrena* does not mean the state; on the contrary, its sole meaning is that it represents a mystical society made up of members who are distinguished by the commitment of their love, not by social or political systems. And Augustine lays out this distinction carefully and unequivocally.

This is not the place to go into a discussion of the complex subject concerning the influence of Greek philosophy on the development of Augustine's thought and his, in turn, on the thought of the Middle Ages.[6] But there is one important aspect of Plato's philosophy that greatly influenced Augustine that we need to have before us as the background for what is to follow. In Greek thought, as we know, there was a preoccupation with the attempt to establish a relationship between the order and constancy of the world of ideas and the flux and impermanence of the world of the senses. That part of Platonism that had the most significance for Augustine was the explanation it offered of reality: its view of an otherworldly source of truth; its view of the dualism of existence—the supernatural or ideal opposed to the phenomenal or sensible world; and its view that the individual must transcend the sensible world to reach the ideal realm. In other words, the theory that reality consists of an "otherworldly" realm and a "this-worldly" realm.[7] Plato's well-known views on this subject can be summarized simply as follows. For Plato there are two realms of being, one the phenomenal realm, and the other the realm of Ideas and Forms. The phenomenal world is characterized by impermanence—things come into being and pass out of being—and the ideal realm is characterized by permanence and timelessness. The ideal realm is the realm of ultimate reality, of pure unchanging "forms" or "ideas" which are absolute and eternal and which constitute an order of reality that transcends earthly existence. This transcendent realm of perfect and fixed eternal "universals," or "essences," stands in contrast to the sensible world where everything is but a reflection of the ideal and where all phenomena are transitory. The sensible world is a manifestation of the realm of the unchanging world of Ideas; it is, therefore, the realm of the ideal which informs and constitutes reality. And, because they are immanent, the unchanging "universals" or "essences" can be known through the faculty of reason by disengaging it from sensible experience. Thus the transcendent world of ultimate reality alone provides certainty; the ideal Forms and Ideas have their own existence and their own order, and they are the source of all other forms and ideas, and of order in the phenomenal world. Platonic otherworldliness thus deals with the idea of a world of eternal essences which correspond to the phenomena of this world.

Augustine accepted totally the Platonic idea of an ideal otherworldly realm. But Augustine modified the notion to make it conform to his Christian beliefs. Accordingly, the conceptual center in Augustinian thought is the idea of a God who brought into being the phenomenal world and all of its creatures, a supreme being who arranged the order of the universe and whose providence guides and directs all creatures. This underlying proposition of creation as the act of the free will and choice of an otherworldly, personal supreme being is sharply different from anything in Plato's thought and, not unexpectedly, it leads to a concept of an otherworldly realm that is unlike Plato's world of Ideas and Forms.[8] In Augustine Plato's transcendent world of universals becomes a completely other and absolutely transcendent realm, and a realm profoundly different in kind from the sensible world. The Augustinian ideal other world is perceived as the realm of a creator-God (rather than as a realm of qualities and values) who alone is supreme ("Since God is the summit of being, that is to say, he *is* supremely and is therefore unchangeable, he granted being to the objects that he created out of nothing, but not the supreme kind of being such as belongs to him"[9]), and with whom those who have been so predestined shall, in an existence beyond historical time, enjoy eternal peace. Augustine's realm of the ideal is, then, completely dissociated from the sensible world; it is a world that is in its characteristics totally different from the categories of human thought and experience. In contrast to Plato's ideal world which becomes intelligible through the faculty of reason, the reality of Augustine's otherworldly realm cannot be known solely through the processes of the mind; rather its existence is accepted, finally, on faith: "Many things whose reason cannot be discovered are still undoubtedly true," and these things "we have no doubt we are bound to believe."[10] There is, then, no correspondence between the supernatural realm and the phenomenal world—on the contrary, there is a distinct dichotomy between them. Thus rather than being a reflection or a manifestation of the ideal realm, this world is, for Augustine, its antithesis.

Now any concept of otherworldliness must always take into account this world, and it must inevitably say something about the nature of the phenomenal world; consequently, it will also make either a direct or an indirect statement about the value of this world. We have seen that for Plato the phenomenal world corresponds in each of its "particulars" to the realm of the ideal. In Platonic thought all of the diverse aspects of nature—physical, moral, aesthetic—are projected into another realm of being where they are exempt from passage and change. Plato's otherworldly realm of Ideas and Forms is, to use Arthur Lovejoy's phrase, a "detemporalized replica of this world."[11] Rather than devaluing this world, Plato's world of Ideas and Forms is, in truth, a glorification of the sensible world. At the same time, the correspondence that Plato establishes between the two realms exalts humankind, for it is through contemplation, that is, through the use of the faculty of reason, that the ideal can be known. And the value of striving to know the truth of the ideal, as Plato demonstrates in the *Republic,* is that it informs us of that which we should aspire to achieve in this world. The Platonic ideal realm is, in brief, instrumental to terrestrial ends, to an ideal in this life, not to an end outside the phenomenal world.

Augustine proposes a quite different point of view. Augustinian eschatology explains the relationship between the ideal realm and this world through the doctrine of divine providence; it describes the sensible world as completely dissociated from, and the antithesis of, the ideal realm; and it characterizes human nature through the tenets of original sin and grace. In Augustine the idealization of the ideal realm is so extreme that his other world goes beyond all modes of human thought and experience, and it is so highly valued that it inherently dismisses this world as having no legitimate value in its own right. Thus for Augustine the dichotomy between the two realms of being is the categorical division between the divine and the created. And the link between the two realms is not intelligibility, as it is with Plato, but grace. The Platonic idea that knowledge of the supernatural can be grasped through intellectual speculation is transformed in Augustine to the idea that knowledge of the actuality of the other world is dependent upon faith. The starting point for Augustine is the rejection of the phenomenal world and the identification of the sole value of existence with a world that is both the antithesis of this world and outside of time. So far as this world is concerned, its value is that it is the preparation for the next; and so far as humankind is concerned, its purpose is to seek redemption from original sin and to strive to achieve salvation through God's grace. The value of striving to know the truth of the ideal otherworldly realm in Augustinian thought, as he demonstrates in *The City of God,* is not that it informs us about an ideal that can be achieved in this world but rather that it reveals what may be attained beyond time. In Greek thought the focus was consistently on what humankind could achieve; in Augustinian thought, as P. R. L. Brown has remarked, the focus is on what we can only hope for in an existence beyond time.[12] In direct contrast to Plato's theory that the ideal realm is instrumental to earthly ends, the Augustinian proposition is that the ideal realm is instrumental to a trans-historical end.

In view of these underlying differences in thought on the value of the otherworldly realm, it is not surprising that we find in Augustine a total departure from the classical notion of order and, in turn, of the role of the state, or *res publica,* in human affairs. Like Plato, Augustine believes in the immutability of an order that acts by law.[13] In Augustine, however, the order of the universe is a providential order arranged by God, who created nature and the human race: "God can create things which are new not to him but to the world, things which were neither created previously nor yet at any time unforeseen by him."[14] Underlying the world of change is an order *(ordo)* which does not admit of change, an order that is abiding and eternal, an order that created the spiritual world and the phenomenal world, an order that is in all creation and which composes part to part "according to the order of nature." Augustine also accepts the Platonic idea that the cosmos is dualistic; but again he departs significantly from Plato in his views on the nature of that dualism. Whereas for Plato dualism is conceived of as constituting spatial and nonspatial realms (the realm of phenomena and the realm of Forms or Ideas) which "exist apart from" each other,[15] in the Augustinian concept of order the universe is pervaded by two modes of being—symbolized by the City of God and the earthly city—that encompass and transcend spatial and nonspatial phenomena; in other words, two realms which co-exist not only in the physical but at the same time in the nonphysical world.[16] In Greek thought, as we have seen, the idea of universal order centered on the relationship between the individual and political order, that is, in the belief in an intrinsic connection between human perfectibility and the *polis;* in Augustinian thought, however, the notion of universal order focuses on the relationship between the individual and two universal societies—the *civitas Dei* and the *civitas terrena.* These two distinctly different yet interacting universal societies form the conceptual center of Augustine's intricate pattern of universal order. Thus whereas Plato in the *Republic* presented a description of an ideal commonwealth—one that is ruled by reason and devoted to reasonable ends—in which the organic relationship between the individual and political order had achieved its ideal fulfillment,[17] Augustine in *The City of God* describes the state of blessed peace and happiness that is the destiny of the members of the City of God.

> How great will be that happiness where there will be no evil, where no good will be hidden, where there will be time for the praises of God, who will be all in all! For I know not what other occupation there can be where no one will be inactive from idleness, and no one will toil because of any lack. Of this I am reminded also by the holy psalm where I read or hear the words: "Blessed are they that dwell in thy house, they shall praise thee for ever and ever." All the limbs and inner organs of the incorruptible body, organs now assigned to various necessary uses, will contribute to the praise of God, for then there will be no necessity, but a happiness that is full, sure, untroubled, eternal.[18]

Because Augustine rejects the classical utopian idea that there is an intimate connection between human perfectibility and the political order, he stresses in *The City of God*, as we saw earlier, that *civitas* or society is not synonymous with *res publica* or the state. Robert Markus and Oliver O'Donovan, among other scholars, have emphasized that while the state, for Augustine, intersects with both the *civitas Dei* and the *civitas terrena*, it nonetheless remains an entity distinctly separate from these two spiritually constituted "cities" or "societies."[19] The Augustinian point of view is that two commitments have produced two cities or societies into which all humankind is divided: the members of the society of God are devoted to divine truth; those of the earthly society reject God and love the things of this world. And central to this theory of two cities is the notion of a society that is at once a mystical community and a temporal community. To put it somewhat differently, in Augustine's scheme the underlying order of the universe manifests itself in two societies, both of which are universal—the human race, in other words, has been divided into two peoples.[20] There is, as we see, a fundamental difference between Plato's doctrine of Ideas or Forms that exist in the spiritual realm of the ideal and the universal and that exist apart from the realm of phenomena, and Augustine's concept of the relationship between the spiritual and phenomenal worlds. For Augustine the "two societies" into which all human creation has been divided exist apart not only from God but also from each other, and each society in turn exists *simultaneously* in both the spiritual and the phenomenal worlds. Platonic dualism in Augustinian thought has taken on another dimension. While the immutable order exists independent of the realm of change there is another kind of dualism *within* the spiritual world and the phenomenal world, and it is this dualism that Augustine distinguishes by the names *"civitas Dei"* and *"civitas terrena."* These two cities, according to Augustine, originated "among [the] angels." Each society is a "social union between [human beings] and angels, so that we are justified in speaking, not of four cities, namely, two of angels and as many of [human beings], but rather of two cities—one of the good and one of the bad, not merely good and bad angels, but good and bad [human beings] as well."[21] The members of the *civitas Dei* in their mortal existence live in "union with the good angels," and those of the *civitas terrena* live in "company with the bad angels." And it is preordained that each of us is a member of either the *civitas Dei* or the *civitas terrena* and that the members of each society belong to that society not only in time but also in eternity.

It is this fundamental proposition in Augustine's thought—that the members of the *civitas terrena* and the *civitas Dei* are intermingled in history—that has led scholars to argue that he has incorporated in his work ideas about a utopian ideal state that we should aspire to achieve while living in time in this world. Since in classical utopianism the state is the means through which humanity's *telos* is made possible, it is important that we understand Augustine's views on the state and the role he believes it has in human affairs. Let us see whether *The City of God* contains a model of an ideal state that human beings should aspire to establish in order to achieve the good life in this world.

Augustine gives his definition of a *res publica* in chapter 21 of book 19. He begins his discussion by arguing against the definition of a people *(populus)* and of a state *(res publica)* given by Scipio in Cicero's *De Republica*. Scipio defines a republic as "a people's estate" and a people as "a numerous gathering united . . . by a common sense of right [i.e., an agreement about justice] and a community of interest."[22] Augustine agrees that a common acknowledgment of right or justice is essential to a true *res publica,* but the way his position differs from Cicero's is revealed in a critical distinction he develops in his argument. According to Augustine, since justice is the distinguishing characteristic or the first condition of a true commonwealth it follows that "where there is no true justice there can be no gathering [of people united by] a common sense of right, and therefore no people as defined by Scipio and Cicero; and if no people, then no people's estate."[23] Augustine states the core of his argument this way: "If, then, a republic is a people's estate, and if that is not a people that is not united . . . by a common sense of right, and if there is no right where there is no justice, then the certain consequence is that where there is no justice there is no state."[24] He then poses his critical distinction: "What sort of justice is it that removes [a person] from the true God?"[25] Thus whereas Augustine accepts the overriding principle that in a true *res publica* each person must be "given their due," for him there is a prior consideration: "Is that assigning to every [individual] their due," he asks, when human beings take themselves from God?[26] The essence of Augustine's argument is that there can be no "justice" in a person who "does not serve God."[27] Therefore although a kind of justice is found in that commonwealth made up of individuals who love and serve God—that is, in that society of individuals who are members of the City of God on earth—because of the fall no earthly state can ever possess or attain true justice: "True justice, however, exists only in that republic whose Founder and Ruler is Christ. . . . True justice resides in that city of which the Holy Scriptures say, 'Glorious things are said of thee, O City of God.'"[28] Thus from the Augustinian point of view no state—whether pagan or Christian—has ever been or can ever be a true *res publica.*

> Therefore where there is no justice whereby the one and most high God rules an obedient city according to his grace, so that it sacrifices to none other save to him only, . . . [where neither the individuals nor the community] live by faith, which works by love, the love whereby [human beings] love God as he should be loved. . . . Where there is no such justice, I say, assuredly there is no gathering of [people] united . . . by a common sense of right and by a community of interest.[29]

In sum, since the *civitas terrena* came into existence because of the fall, since the *civitas terrena* and the *civitas Dei* are intermingled in history, since the fulfillment of the *civitas Dei* is possible only in a life beyond historical time, and since this life is for the members of the *civitas Dei* but a "pilgrimage" of the soul in the journey toward redemption, it is axiomatic that true justice, hence a true *res publica,* cannot, according to Augustine's universal theory of history, be established in the earthly world.

Are we therefore to conclude from this that Augustine agrees with those early theologians who held that there is no fundamental relationship between the citizen and the state? Tertullian, for example, argued not only that the state had no legitimate claim on the individual but also that the interests of the individual and the interests of the state were inherently antithetical. "What concord," Tertullian asks, "is there between the Academy and the Church? . . . Our instruction comes from the Porch of Solomon who taught that the Lord should be sought in simplicity of heart. Away with all attempts to produce a mottled Christianity of Stoic, Platonic, and dialectic composition."[30] Does Augustine also believe that the state must be rejected absolutely? that the state has no specific role in human history? that the interests of the individual and the interests of the state are inherently antithetical? The fact is that although Augustine believes that establishing a true *res publica* is impossible, he develops at the same time a theory about the role and function of the state that stands in direct opposition to Tertullian's attitude. The question of what Augustine's views are on the place the state has in human affairs is resolved when we realize that the answer lies in the principle that the two cities "are interwoven, as it were, and blended together in this transitory age."[31] The state is thus itself a part of God's divine providence and, as such, has a definite purpose and specific role in human history. Indeed, Augustine wonders how anyone can believe that "he would have excluded from the laws of his providence the kingdoms of [human beings] and their dominations and servitudes."[32] On the contrary, he says, "let us not ascribe the power of granting kingdoms and empires to any except the true God. To the religious alone he grants happiness in the kingdom of heaven, but earthly kingdoms he grants both to the religious and the irreligious."[33]

Augustine makes clear that he does not reject the state; rather he conceives of it as part of God's universe and therefore as an integral part of human history. To resolve the problem raised by the idea on the one hand that a true *res publica* cannot be achieved in this life, and on the other the proposition that there exists an intrinsic relationship between the citizen and the state, Augustine gives an alternative definition of a *res publica* in which he makes a critical substitution of terms—he rejects the Ciceronian definition of justice and argues that a people is "a large gathering of rational beings united . . . by their agreement about the objects of their love."[34] And for Augustine humankind can have only one "common agreement"—to love and honor God. If, however, the meaning of existence is an ultimate *telos* outside of time and if the only common agreement human beings have is to love and honor God, what function, then, can the state have? Although he devotes considerable attention to this complex subject in his text, Augustine's argument can be summarized this way: the function of the state is to maintain peace, and the state fulfills this purpose because it has the authority and the power to maintain order.[35] Order then results in peace. The virtue of the temporal state is that it provides and maintains a "remedial order" that makes possible a "temporal peace." And although a temporal peace is not comparable to the true peace found only in the City of God beyond time, as Augustine explains, it "must not be rejected . . . since so long as the two cities are intermingled we also profit by the peace of Babylon."[36]

Thus in Augustinian thought a state with the authority to maintain order and peace is divinely ordained and the individual's responsibility to the state is to be obedient. In her essay on early Christian political thought, Elaine Pagels points out that Augustine, in dramatic contrast to the views of many of his predecessors, "emphasized that humankind was irreparably damaged by the fall" and, as a consequence, "humankind has wholly lost its original capacity for self-government." Augustine, she adds, "draws so drastic a picture of the effects of Adam's sin that he embraces human government, even when tyrannical, as the indispensable defense against the forces sin has unleashed in human nature."[37] In contrast to the Platonic idea that justice is the sum of all virtue, and that it is founded on will and reason, obedience is the virtue, according to Augustine, that is "guardian of all virtues in a rational creature, inasmuch as we have been naturally so created that it is advantageous for us to be submissive but ruinous to follow our own will and not the will of the creator."[38] In Augustinian thought the *sole* value of the state is that it ensures order and therefore peace in the temporal world: "Every use of temporal things is related to the enjoyment of earthly peace in the earthly city, while in the heavenly city it is related to the enjoyment of everlasting peace."[39] And that is why the citizen is impelled to accept and obey the laws of civil authority—political and social arrangements are of divine rather than human origin and in being subservient to the state the individual is, in fact, being subservient to the will of God.

In sum, the dominant idea in the Augustinian concept of order is that the state is divinely appointed and is that part of the total *ordo* of creation which directs human beings toward their trans-historical end. According to Augustine, if God had not created the state anarchy would reign and people would destroy each other because of their propensity toward "love of self" rather than "love of God." The corrective to this inevitability is a state conceived of as a remedial instrument that is itself part of God's divine scheme. Sheldon Wolin summarizes Augustine's attitude about the state this way: "To the degree that a political society promoted peace it was good; to the degree that it embodied a well-ordered concord among its members it was even better; to the extent that it encouraged a Christian life and avoided a conflict in loyalties between religious and political obligations, it had fulfilled its role within the universal scheme."[40] Briefly, even a state alienated from God—as all earthy states must be—is absolutely necessary; and because the state is part of God's divine scheme its instruments are God's earthly instruments for our possible redemption.

We have agreed that classical utopianism is a mode of thought that deals with humanity's temporal condition and that the intention of classical utopias is to offer ideas concerning a perceived possibility of achieving the good life in this world. In direct contrast, the fundamental proposition in Augustine's thought is the doctrine of divine providence, and in his explication of this thesis he develops a comprehensive philosophy of universal history the ultimate end of which is the fulfillment of God's promise to humankind, the attainment of an ideal supernatural state of existence. Thus whereas the issue from the classical utopist's point of view is whether the individual will serve the ends of the state toward achieving the utopian *telos,* from the Augustinian viewpoint the issue is whether we will serve the ends of eternity. At no point in his voluminous work does Augustine talk about specific social and political arrangements. The truth is that the issues of central importance to the classical utopist—political, social, and economic arrangements—are deliberately eschewed by Augustine. At the same time, none of the central ideas he develops in his analysis—two societies, predestination, grace, divine providence—plays any role in classical utopianism. The overriding value in classical utopias is that the state is the means by which human beings may possibly achieve the good life. In *The City of God,* on the other hand, the emphasis is on the individual, not on society; it is on the integration of the individual with God, not on an integration with social institutions. To put it another way, self-realization in *The City of God* is shaped by an affinity with the spiritual life; in utopia it is derived from an active involvement with social institutions. Thus the architectonic order of utopian social structures has no place in *The City of God* where the quest for redemption is based on the idea of a life free from complex political influences. Whereas in classical utopianism there exists an intimate connection between the political order and collective fulfillment, for Augustine the peace and order the state maintains provides external conditions that are conducive to the individual's seeking personal salvation through the grace of God. In Augustine's view, the ideal temporal state is distinguished not by its political structures and social arrangements but rather by whether it fulfills the standard that "the rulers do not force [people] to commit unholy and unjust deeds."[41]

Augustine argues that the appointed end of the *civitas Dei* is an ideal life where we will enjoy everlasting and perfect peace, no longer subject to the wretchedness of mortal life. In striking contrast to the classical utopist's description of an ideal organization of things in the temporal world, here the concept of an ideal existence is a vision of a mystical or spiritual state of being—in no sense is it an idealization of temporal life. For Augustine the attainment of an "ideal life" is strictly limited to an existence outside of historical time and human events.[42] Throughout the development of his argument Augustine consistently draws a distinction between what is possible in history and what is possible outside of the temporal world. And while classical utopias too are conceived of as transcending historical periods, they do not transcend historical time. On the other hand it is the belief that human history has a *telos* outside of time that lies at the heart of Augustine's work, and he never allows us to lose sight of this argument. Given Augustine's own propositions, we can see that *The City of God* and classical utopianism are based on different, indeed conflicting, premises. From the standpoint of utopia, *The City of God* offers an interpretation of the human condition and the temporal world that inevitably results in a rejection of the basic tenets and the ordering paradigms associated with classical utopianism. In short, not only is *The City of God* not an example of utopian writing, it is, in truth, an injunction against utopian speculation.

Chapter 2

Sacred and Secular Order: Aquinas and the Body Politic

*I*n the previous chapter I attempted to show how in Augustinian thought the concept of order was recast in such a way that the earlier idea about the relationship between order in the temporal and supertemporal realms was rejected and, as we have seen, replaced by Augustine with a new vision of order—one that served to idealize the supernatural realm of order and, concurrently, to devalue the integrity of temporal order and to simultaneously reshape the role humankind has in establishing and maintaining order in the temporal realm. The culmination of Augustine's system—with its underlying proposition of a providential plan controlling human destiny and its reliance upon faith rather than reason—was to spell the end to a concept of order as the product of human nature, and hence to classical utopianism, and to substitute in its place a doctrine of theological order that made temporal order subservient to an other-worldly personal God.

In contrast, as we shall see, Thomas Aquinas proposed substantially different ideas about the order of the universe, the nature of human beings, and the role of the state in human affairs. As Paul Weithman, among others, has observed, "the rediscovery of Aristotelian moral thought in the thirteenth century influenced medieval political theory profoundly. Recovery of Aristotle's *Politics*, for example, made available to political theorists of the period analyses of political institutions that differed significantly from those they found in Patristic sources. Differences between Aristotle's views and those of Augustine were especially striking. Thomas Aquinas was one of the

31

first and most influential of the thirteenth-century Aristotelians."[1] For purposes of our study, the most important features of Aquinas's thought are his emphasis on the integrity of a rational order in the temporal realm, his reaffirmation that human beings are by nature political beings, and his view that the state is the means to achieve our natural fulfillment. Rejecting the earlier view of the state as a product of sin, Aquinas argues, as we will see, that the state or political order is founded upon human nature itself. I have mentioned that classical utopian speculation is directly linked to notions of order. If we want to understand how Aquinas's thought influenced the tradition of classical utopianism, we need to explore his views on the order of the universe, and, more specifically, his ideas on the place the state has within this scheme of universal order. We shall see that while Aquinas himself does not directly engage in classical utopian discourse, he offered an interpretation of the order of the universe and of human nature that was a primary influence on the reappearance in the fourteenth century of classical utopian thought. In brief, the emphasis here is on a consideration of the contrast in outlook between Aquinas and Augustine with respect to their views on order and the nature of human nature. This approach will more clearly show that the final result of much of Aquinas's thought is that it served, in the utopian tradition, as the bridge between Plato's *Republic* and the rehabilitation in the late Medieval period of classical utopianism.

Thus, we find that whereas in Augustine's view order is based upon contrast and dichotomy, in Aquinas the concept of order is founded on the idea of two hierarchically different yet complementary orders: the natural order and the supernatural order. Like Augustine's, the Thomistic notion of order is of a system that serves to organize realms of being into a hierarchy of structures imposed by divine providence. And again, as in Augustine's system, in Aquinas's thought God has created two realms of being. But whereas for Augustine there is, on the one hand, the dualism of the spiritual realm and the phenomenal realm, and on the other the dualism of two modes of being *within* the spiritual and phenomenal worlds which he distinguishes as the mystical societies of the *civitas Dei* and *civitas terrena,* for Aquinas there are only two orders, the natural order and the supernatural order. And in Aquinas the natural and supernatural orders are not opposite orders in conflict with each other but, rather, they are *different* orders with different operating principles. As he explains, in a hierarchy of orders

> one hierarchy means one rule, i.e., a single group organized under the governance of one ruler. Any group, however, would not be organized but chaotic if within it there were not different orders. The very meaning of a hierarchy, then, demands a distinction of orders.[2]

> A hierarchy means a sacred rule. Two elements are denoted in the term "rule," the ruler and the many persons joined under him. Since God is the ruler not only over all the angels, but over [humankind] and every creature, from this standpoint there is the one hierarchy comprising all angels and all rational creatures as capable of sharing in the sacred. . . . However, if we look at a regimen from the standpoint of the many organized under the ruler, then it is one to the extent that the many are governable in the one way. Those who are not governable in the one way come under different rules. . . . Now it is obvious that [human beings] and angels receive divine enlightenment differently, since angels receive it in its pure intelligibility, [human beings] under material symbols. . . . Therefore the human hierarchy has to be different from the angelic.[3]

In contrast to Augustine, Aquinas makes a distinction between the "human and the angelic hierarchy," and this distinction results from the fact that a group "would not be organized but chaotic if within it there were not different orders."

The conceptual element that enables Aquinas to achieve a reconciliation between the dualism of opposing orders is his view of the relationship between grace and nature. From Aquinas's point of view grace does not do away with nature but rather perfects it: "Thus we must say for the knowledge of any truth, [human beings] need divine assistance so that [their] intellect may be moved by God to actualize itself. [They] do not however need a new light, supplementing [their] natural light in order to know the truth in all cases, but only in certain cases which transcend natural knowledge."[4] Accordingly, although there are different operating principles in nature and grace, these principles do not oppose each other. As Walter Ullmann has observed, "the traditional gulf between nature and grace was bridged by Thomas. There was no ambiguity in his thought about the efficacy of nature itself and of natural law—both did and could operate without any revelation or grace or divine assistance, because they followed their own inherent laws and these latter had nothing to do with grace."[5] It is this outlook that made it possible for Aquinas to conceive of a dualism of two hierarchically different orders which, although they operate on different principles, are not opposed to each other since they function on two different levels.

A major tenet of Aristotelian doctrine that was of singular importance to Aquinas was the view of the relationship between nature and the state. To demonstrate the similarity between their views on this subject, we need to first examine the Aristotelian argument. In Aristotelian thought nature is conceived of in teleological terms: "Nature makes nothing incomplete," and "Nature makes nothing in vain." Thus "what each thing is when fully developed, we call its nature."[6] For Aristotle the laws of nature brought forth human reason; reason, in other words, is linked with nature. Whereas what distinguishes animals is that they merely "obey their instincts," what characterizes human beings is the faculty of reason by which "the end toward which nature strives" is expressed.[7] Aristotle's ideas on the relationship between the laws of nature and human reason culminated in his view of the state as the product of nature, the result of the working of the laws of nature, not the result of an act of creation. The laws of nature determine that we live in a self-sufficient, autonomous community—the state—within which we can achieve our perfection. "Since the end of individuals and of states is the same, . . . the state exists for the sake of a perfect and self-sufficing life. . . . The end is the good life and [the state] is the means towards it."[8] In sum, since reason is the instrument through which nature operates, the state is the natural product of the laws of nature. Thus it is the citizens of the state who articulate the will of nature and who, therefore, possess the natural right to participate in the government of the state. Aristotle, however, draws a distinction between the individual and the citizen, and this conceptualization is one that Aquinas follows very closely. According to Aristotle, "it is evident that the good citizen need not of necessity possess the virtue which makes a good [person]."[9] Thus in Aristotelian thought the citizen is seen as governed by principles which relate to the political order, whereas the individual operates on principles related to ethics. This dichotomy between the person and the citizen is of crucial importance in the thought of Aquinas.

The leading idea that Aquinas derives from Aristotle is the view that we are by nature political beings. Aquinas returns again and again to this theme. In one place he says there is a threefold order in human nature—divine law, reason, and political authority. If we were by nature solitary animals, the order of reason and that of divine law would have been sufficient. But since we are "social and political animals, . . . a third order is required whereby [we] are directed in relation to others among whom [we] must live."[10] Aquinas's doctrine of the political nature of human beings is based on the idea that because human beings operate not by instinct but by reason, social organization is necessary in order that they may achieve their purpose as rational beings. Unlike Augustine, who argues that the state has its origins in human sinfulness, for Aquinas the state has its origins in human reason. Dino Bigongiari rightly points out that in Aquinas's view because human beings "operate, not by instinct, but by reason, social organization is indispensable. . . . By endowing human beings with reason and at the same time depriving them of instinct and of an available ready-made supply of the necessities of life, God decreed that they should be political animals."[11] This interdependence of reason and social organization is emphasized by Aquinas.

> [Human beings], who act by intelligence, have a destiny to which all . . . life and activities are directed; for it is clearly the nature of intelligent beings to act with some end in view. . . . When we consider all that is necessary to human life, it becomes clear that [human beings] are naturally social and political animals, destined more than all other animals to live in community. . . . Other animals have a natural instinct for what is useful or hurtful to them. . . . We, on the other hand, have a natural knowledge of life's necessities only in a general way. Being gifted with reason [we] must use it to pass from

such universal principles to the knowledge of what in particular concerns [our] well-being. Reasoning thus, however, no one [person] could attain all necessary knowledge. Instead, nature has destined [us] to live in society. . . . The [bond] of society being thus natural and necessary, it follows with equal necessity that there must be some principle of government within the society.[12]

Because we are born with a common vague notion, rather than a particularized instinct, of what is necessary in life, we apply reason to universal principles in order to learn what in particular concerns our well-being. But since we cannot individually acquire all the knowledge that we need, nature has destined us to live in collaboration with others. That it is inherent in our nature to live in cooperation with others is proven by the fact that human beings alone are endowed with reason and with the capacity for speech. It is nature, then, which determines that we are "destined more than all other animals to live in community"; and as reason is the principle in human nature which directs us toward our end, the state is the directive principle in the community which guides "social beings" toward their *telos.*

For Aquinas human beings are political animals because they are by nature social beings; as members of human society they form associations to ensure their well-being. And of all the associations they can form, the most perfect is the state for it alone has the capacity of ensuring the achievement of their needs.

Among communities there are different grades and orders, the highest being the political community, which is so arranged to satisfy all the needs of human life, and which is, in consequence, the most perfect. For since all things which serve [our] needs have the fulfillment of this purpose as their end, and since ends are more important than the means thereto, it follows that this unity which we call a city takes preeminence over all smaller unities which the human reason can know and construct.[13]

The state, then, is the most perfect of all human associations. And as a product of nature, on the one hand, and as an end in itself, on the other, the state has its own natural laws of operation. The state thus pursues aims that are inherent in the nature of the individual. These aims, however, can be achieved only if there is a distinction between the natural order and the supernatural order, a distinction between the citizen and the Christian.

> We should bear in mind that [dominion or authority] is an institution of human law, whereas the distinction between the faithful and infidels is by divine law. Now divine law, which is from grace, does not do away with human law, which is from natural reason. Consequently the distinction between the faithful and the infidels, considered in itself, does not cancel the dominion or authority of infidels over the faithful.[14]

In Aquinas's view the state has a value of its own, independent of religion. The state is the product of nature; the Church is the product of divinity. The state is a matter for the citizen only; the Church is a matter for the Christian only. Although both the state and the Church are manifestations of the hierarchical order imposed on all things by divine providence, the nature of a hierarchy requires, as we have seen, a "distinction of orders," and orders that are "diverse do not come together"; thus, according to Aquinas, "there must needs be a distinction between the human and the angelic hierarchy." Now this is precisely the kind of distinction that Augustine does not make in his definition of a society. On the contrary, as discussed in the previous chapter, for Augustine the society of the *civitas terrena* and the society of the *civitas Dei* include both the human race and angels.

Thus Aquinas gives the term *civitas*, or society, a new meaning. In the Thomistic conception of the order of the universe people do not share membership in universal or mystical societies. Rather, they belong to a natural society that is the product of natural reason. If the individual should also be a Christian, then that person is also a member of the *corpus mysticum*. The two types of membership that Aquinas identifies are the *civitas* and the *corpus mysticum*, both of which are given the name of "perfect communities," one the natural, the other the supernatural. But both of these communities, since they function on different operating principles, are self-sufficient and independent, and the Christian owes allegiance to each of them.

Both the spiritual and the temporal power derive from the divine power; consequently the temporal power is subject to the spiritual only to the extent that this is so ordered by God; namely in those matters which affect the salvation of the soul. And in these matters the spiritual power is to be obeyed before the temporal. In those matters, however, which concern the civil welfare, the temporal power should be obeyed rather than the spiritual, according to what we are told in St. Matthew (XXII, 21), "Render unto Caesar the things that are Caesar's."[15]

In contrast to Augustine's idea that the state is a consequence of original sin, Aquinas's attitude is that the state is founded upon human nature itself: "The fact that [we] are by nature social animals . . . has as a consequence the fact that [we] are destined by nature to form part of a community which makes a full and complete life possible."[16] As Gordon Leff has said, for Aquinas "there was no need to seek an historical justification for the state, it was organically part of human nature. Sin became merely a by-product of human imperfection to explain injustice, not the state itself."[17] Henry Parkes also remarks that Aquinas's view of human nature, unlike Augustine's, places little emphasis on original sin. Parkes notes that in Aquinas's view human beings do not "desire evil, which is essentially a negation; and if a [person] is guilty of evil, it is because of a disorder in their desires rather than from positive depravity. . . . [In Aquinas's words]: 'Never would evil be sought after, not even as an accident, unless the good that accompanies the evil were more desired than the good of which the evil is the privation.' This optimism extends to Thomas's political views. . . . The laws of the state derive their authority from conformity with the God-created law of nature and reason."[18]

The difference between the prevailing Augustinian viewpoint and Aquinas's outlook is the difference between a system of order that inherently rejects the value of the phenomenal world and substitutes in its place an otherworldly ideal realm of existence; and a system of order that emphasizes the natural necessity of the temporal world on the one hand, and the idea that the temporal world has as its goal its own perfection on the other. And Aquinas achieved this reaffirmation of the value of the temporal realm through his conceptualization of a dichotomy between the natural order and the supernatural order, and through the distinction he makes between the citizen and the Christian. By thus absorbing Aristotle's ideas on nature and on human beings as political animals, Aquinas "effected in the public sphere . . . the re-birth of the citizen who since classical times had been hibernating."[19] And the reaffirmation of the concept of human beings as political animals resulted in the appearance of a philosophy of politics. In Aquinas's words:

> Those human sciences which are about the things of nature are speculative, while those which are concerned with the things made by [human beings] are practical sciences. . . . If we are to perfect the science of human wisdom, or philosophy, it is necessary to give an explanation of all that can be understood by reason. That unity which we call the city is subject to the judgment of reason. It is necessary, then, for the completeness of philosophy, to institute a discipline which will study the city, and such a discipline is called politics or the science of statecraft.[20]

Sheldon Wolin summarizes the dramatic impact of Aquinas's political ideas this way: "In insisting, as Thomas did, upon the vital role of the political order, in seeking to define the distinctive laws by which it was ruled, the unique common good which it served, and the kind of prudence proper to its life, there was a heavy price to be paid, even though the terms were not fully revealed for several centuries. Thomas had not only restored the political order to repute; he had given it a sharpness of identity, a clarity of character, that had been lacking for several centuries."[21] In sum, the reassertion in Aquinas of the idea of the political nature of human beings led to a renewal of the classical belief in the harmonious integration of the individual with the political order. Political philosophy, according to Aquinas, is the study of that knowledge which concerns itself with the government of the state, and it has its own intrinsic value because it is the expression of a natural order.

Before the notion that humankind can control and direct events in the temporal world could take hold, however, a greater demarcation had to be made concerning the relationship between the natural order and the supernatural order. For it is clear that while in Aquinas's thought the state is viewed as self-sufficient and independent, it is, finally, only relatively autonomous. In his doctrine of the duality of existence, based on the idea of the dual directions of the natural order and the supernatural order, Aquinas consistently maintains the primacy of the supernatural order: the ultimate purpose of reason is to support faith; the ultimate value of natural law is that it participates in eternal law; and the ultimate worth of the state is that it shares in that hierarchical order imposed on all things by divine providence. The natural order is a secondary cause and only an instrument. As A. P. D'Entréves says, "the natural order, which comprises and sufficiently justifies political experience, is for St. Thomas only a condition and a means for the recognition of a higher order, as natural law is but a part of the eternal law of God. . . . Nature requires to be perfected by grace. The action of the state, as part of the natural order, must be considered in the general frame of the divine direction of the world, and is entirely subservient to that direction."[22] Although nature is no longer regarded as depraved and the state is no longer spoken of as merely remedial, in Aquinas's thought there are still two orders of membership, and it is the transpolitical that is supreme.

In this vein we need to remember that the transition from an otherworldly to a this-worldly orientation, from Augustine's eschatological "ideal society" to Aquinas's views on the political nature of human beings, goes beyond a shift in worldview perspective concerning the idea of order. Bound up with the revision of thought on the relationship between the temporal realm and the supernatural realm was a fundamental change in outlook regarding the connection between faith and reason.[23] Aquinas made a supreme effort to synthesize the two main traditions inherited from the Middle Ages—the classical thought of Plato and Aristotle, with the Christian teachings of the Scriptures and Augustine. And one of the major ideas he introduced in order to achieve this synthesis was his view of faith and reason as distinct and yet complementary. But while in Aquinas reason is clearly given an unprecedented status, the basis of his system is, nevertheless, that reason is aided by "divine grace"; faith, to put it another way, supplements reason. According to Aquinas, all things proceed from, and are sustained by, divine providence. Hence, even though for Aquinas divine providence manifests itself in two distinctly different orders, the natural order and the supernatural order, the former is not separate from the latter; on the contrary, the natural order completes that order that he says is imposed on all things by divine providence. The temporal world and reason are linked to the supernatural realm and they are, ultimately, governed by supernatural law and faith. Accordingly, the truth of any proposition, for Aquinas, depends, finally, not upon its correspondence with reason and natural law, but upon its being compatible with faith and eternal law.[24] For Aquinas faith is directed toward manifesting the truth of revelation; so far as knowledge is concerned, its chief aim is to show that reason leads to faith. Typical of thirteenth-century thought, Aquinas holds to the idea that faith is, ultimately, the guiding principle in human affairs.

Nonetheless, Aquinas's philosophy, in its views on the distinction between the natural order and the supernatural order, and in the distinction he made between the truths of reason and the truths of faith, easily lent itself to speculation about an absolute dichotomy between this world and any "other world" that could be conceived. And such speculation soon emerged. As one commentator puts it, "the great system-builders of the thirteenth century, despite their relatively liberal and optimistic conceptions of human nature, were attempting to close doors. Having carried the effort to rationalize theology to its farthest-possible limits, they were followed in the fourteenth century by thinkers who affirmed that faith and reason were ultimately irreconcilable."[25] And as Ullmann argues, "this appeared as the thesis that there was a natural law which was in any case valid and persuasive enough without any recourse to divinity, simply because the natural law was reasonable in itself."[26] It is this outlook—the view that human beings are endowed by nature with the capacity to create an ordered temporal world without reference to the idea that they are directed in this effort by a supernatural realm of order—that we find at the core of classical utopian thought. The next chapter will examine two important fourteenth-century works that show the role Aquinas's thought played in giving shape to three ideas significant to the reappearance of classical utopianism—the notion of a fully autonomous temporal order, the idea that natural law functions without divine interference, and the concept that truth is not one but two.[27] Dante's *De Monarchia* and Marsilius of Padua's *Defensor Pacis* foreshadow the end of those modes of thought which propose that there exists an intrinsic relationship between temporal order and the order of a supernatural other world, a fundamental connection between faith and reason, and a direct link between natural law and divine eternal law.

Chapter 3

Redeeming Utopia: Dante's *De Monarchia* and Marsilius's *Defensor Pacis*

As the doctrine of truth as twofold gained favor among four-teenth-century Christian philosophers, there developed a more emphatic emphasis on the proposition that philosophy was totally independent of theology and that the temporal realm was entirely separate from the supernatural realm. What distinguished fourteenth-century philosophers from earlier ones was their insistence on *disengaging* reason completely from faith and, at the same time, dissociating the phenomenal world from a hierarchical system of universal order. Duns Scotus, among others,[1] rejected Aquinas's notion that faith and reason are complementary. Scotus's view is that there can be no rational explanation of divine providence; reason is limited to knowledge of the phenomenal world and it cannot confirm revelation. Theological truths, since they are incapable of demonstration by natural perceptions, lie outside the realm of rational comprehension. Revelation, then, is strictly a matter of faith. For Duns Scotus the connection that Aquinas had made between faith and reason was abandoned, and in its place he proposed the idea that "each is self-contained. . . . The natural and the supernatural are not merely on different planes but without a meeting-point; since they deal with different truths they cannot inform one another."[2] In Duns Scotus the emphasis is on the difference rather than on the harmony between faith and reason. Faith and reason are two entirely separate realms of understanding: faith deals with supernatural truths, reason concerns itself with natural experience. Rather than attempting, as Aquinas had attempted, to reconcile theology with the demands of rational inquiry, Duns Scotus broke the link between the truths of revelation and those of natural knowledge. He resolved the conflict between two incompatible orders—the natural realm and the supernatural realm—by proposing that truth of revelation and truth of reason are two distinctly different kinds of truths—they do not inform each other, and they must be kept separate. Once the attempt to reconcile theological doctrine and natural knowledge was abandoned, the characteristic feature of thought became the notion of truth as not one but two.[3] The effect of this shift in perspective was a revolution in thought in the interpretation of the individual's relation to the natural order. As we shall see, the central idea in both Dante's *De Monarchia* and Marsilius of Padua's *Defensor Pacis* is that the temporal world functions independently of divine providence, and that human reason alone can lead to the fulfillment of one's natural end in this world.

Dante's aim in *De Monarchia* is not to discuss the way in which divine providence operates, as was the case with Augustine in *De Civitate Dei,* but rather to explain the function and purpose of temporal government. His concern, he says, "is with politics, with the very source and principle of all right politics, and *since all political matters are in our control,* it is clear that our present concern is not aimed primarily at thought but at action"[4] [emphasis added]. Dante thus directs his attention to the proper order of things in the temporal world, a world that humankind can control.

De Monarchia is divided into three books with chapter divisions. In Book I, Dante argues that the world should be united under one sovereign rule. For Dante, the aim of humanity in the temporal world is the realization of its full potential, and since our potential "can not be completely actualized in a single [person] or in any of the particular communities of [people], there must be a multitude in [humankind] through whom this whole power can be actualized"; accordingly, "the proper work of [humankind] taken as a whole is to exercise continually its entire capacity for intellectual growth, first, in theoretical matters, and, secondarily, as an extension of theory, in practice."[5] And for Dante, too, civic peace is a necessary requirement for the realization of one's human potential, which is, in Dante's view, the realization of our intellectual potentialities. As he puts it, because "individual [persons] find that they grow in prudence and wisdom when they can sit quietly, it is evident that [humankind], too, is most free and easy to carry on its work when it enjoys the quiet and tranquillity of peace. . . . It is clear that of all the things that have been ordained for our happiness, the greatest is universal peace."[6] Peace is thus indispensable to our well-being. And peace is attainable only in a universal empire, or "world-government," that is ruled by a single authority or "emperor." Further, since God is the first cause of all creation, humanity achieves its goal when it most "resembles" God.

> The whole universe is nothing but a kind of imprint of the divine goodness. Therefore, [humankind] exists at its best when it resembles God as much as it can. [Humankind] resembles God most when it is most unified, for the true ground of unity exists in Him alone. And [humankind] is most one when it is unified into a single whole; which is possible only when it submits wholly to a single government. . . . Therefore [humankind] in submitting to a single government most resembles God and most nearly exists according to the divine intention, which is the same as enjoying well-being.[7]

The world needs a universal government headed by a monarch who would ensure peace among all peoples and ensure the conditions that make it possible for them to achieve their full potential.

In Book II, Dante argues that since the Roman empire was the only true government that ever existed—"both human reason and divine authority show that the Roman Empire existed by right"[8]—the universal monarchy must be Roman. For Dante, the only time in history when the world enjoyed "the blessing of world peace and tranquillity" was during the reign of Caesar Augustus. To summarize Dante's argument: the Roman people were a most noble people,[9] Roman rule was for the common good,[10] the Romans sought to bring universal peace to the world,[11] and the Roman capacity to rule proves that its rule was a natural order.[12]

It is in Book III of *Monarchia* that Dante sets forth his crucial argument that temporal authority comes directly from God but that it is entirely independent of spiritual authority. He asks "whether the authority for world-government comes directly from God or through some other."[13] And he answers with his claim that human beings have two natures—one physical and one spiritual—and that these natures are independent of each other.

> Two-fold, therefore, are the ends which unerring Providence has ordained for [humankind]: the bliss of this life, which consists in the functioning of [our] own powers, and which is typified by the earthly Paradise; and the bliss of eternal life, which consists in the enjoyment of that divine vision to which we cannot attain by our own powers, except they be aided by the divine light, and this state is made intelligible by the celestial Paradise. These two states of bliss, like two different goals, we must reach by different ways. For we come to the first as we follow the philosophical teachings, applying them according to our moral and intellectual capacities; and we come to the second as we follow the spiritual teachings which transcend human reason according to our theological capacities.[14]

Human beings have two goals in this life—a secular one, to achieve happiness in this world, and a spiritual one, to achieve the ultimate good of eternal felicity. These are two separate and distinct goals and they are achieved through different means. Human happiness is acquired through reason; celestial happiness is acquired by the will yielding to faith. Thus, for Dante, reason alone makes it possible to achieve temporal happiness.

The main idea in the *Monarchia* that we want to focus on here is the view it presents of the independence of the temporal order from any hierarchical system of supernatural order. Like Aristotle and Aquinas, Dante believes that human beings are by nature social and political animals and that the state, or from his point of view the "universal monarchy," has a rational and natural foundation.

> An individual has one purpose, a family another, a neighborhood another, a city another, a state another, and finally there is another for all of [humankind]. . . . We should know, in this

connection, that God and nature make nothing in vain, and that whatever is produced serves some function. For the intention of any act of creation, if it is really creative, is not merely to produce the existence of something but to produce the proper functioning of that existence. . . . Hence, a proper functioning does not exist for the sake of the being which functions, but rather the being exists for the sake of its function. There is therefore some proper function for the whole of [humankind] as an organized multitude which can not be achieved by any single [person], or family, or neighborhood, or city, or state.[15]

Dante's emphasis is, on the one hand, consistently on the universality of the human condition and, on the other, on the idea that happiness in this life is achieved by the exercise, growth and actualization of our intellectual powers. It is determined by nature that this is humanity's purpose and its final destiny in the temporal realm. The collective goal of *humana civilitas* is the achievement of this ideal. What the proper function for the whole of humankind might be would be clear enough if we could see what the basic capacity of the whole of humanity is. Dante sets forth his ideas on this inherent capacity in detail in chapter 3 of Book I.

Now I would say that no capacity which several different species have in common can be the basic power of any one of them. For in that case the basic capacity, which characterized a species, would be the same for several species, which is impossible. Accordingly, [our] basic capacity is not mere being, for we share being with the elements; nor is it to be compounded, for this is found in minerals, too; nor is it to be alive, for so are plants; nor is it to be sensitive, for other animals share this power; but it is to be sensitive to intellectual growth, for this trait is not found in beings either above or below [human beings]. . . . Therefore, it is clear that [our] basic capacity is to have a potentiality or power for being intellectual. And since this power can not be completely actualized in a single [person] or in any of the particular communities of [people] above mentioned, there must be a multitude in [humankind] through whom this whole power can be actualized;

> just as there must be a multitude of created beings to manifest
> adequately the whole power of prime matter, otherwise there
> would have to be a power distinct from prime matter, which is
> impossible.[16]

Everything, Dante states, is ordered toward a goal or "finis" that it strives to achieve and everything has a proper function or "operatio" by means of which to reach this end. Our temporal "finis" is to attain well-being and happiness in this world and the "operatio" through which this goal is achieved is the collective faculty of reason possessed by the whole of humankind which enables us to attain our own individual well-being and happiness and, in turn, participate in the achievement of the well-being and happiness of others.

Since humanity's human potential can only be realized in a well-ordered society, order in the temporal realm is the product of the rational nature of human beings. There is a supernatural order that exists in its own right, but there is also a distinct and separate temporal order that is the result of human reason and human nature.

> I maintain that from the fact that the moon does not shine
> brightly unless it receives light from the sun, it does not follow
> that the moon itself depends on the sun. For one must keep in
> mind that the being of the moon is one thing, its power another, and its functioning a third. In its being the moon is in
> no way dependent on the sun, and not even in its power and
> functioning, strictly speaking, for its motion comes directly
> from the prime mover. . . . In like manner, I maintain, temporal power receives from spiritual power neither its being, nor
> its power or authority, nor even its functioning, strictly speaking, but what it receives is the light of grace.[17]

Although the temporal order may be enhanced by the "light of grace," it receives from spiritual power neither its being, nor its power or authority. As we have seen, Dante's view of the autonomy of the political order is based on the idea that the individual aspires to two beatitudes, one on earth, the other in heaven. The attainment of the "bliss of this life" and the "bliss of eternal life" is, then, accomplished by different means. The former is reached through the exercise of the "moral and intellectual capacities"; the latter is achieved by "following the spiritual teachings which transcend human reason." The two ends that "unerring Providence" has ordained for the individual are independent and the paths to their attainment have nothing in common. The temporal world and its authority "come directly, without intermediary," from God.

A fundamental task confronting humankind is the search for the truth of the right order of human affairs as determined by human reason and as it enhances the actualization of our full potential in the temporal realm. And, as we have noted above, it is determined by nature that the achievement of our full potential in the temporal realm is a collective endeavor. In striving toward the happiness that is our temporal end each individual person has a particular purpose but these individual purposes are ultimately linked to the higher good of the happiness that is ordered for all humankind.

> Whatever relation a part bears to its whole, the structure of that part must bear to the total structure. But a part is related to the whole as to its end or greatest good. Hence we must conclude that the goodness of the partial structure cannot exceed the goodness of the total structure, rather the contrary. Now since there is a double structure among things . . . it follows the structure which makes a unity out of parts is better than the other structure, for it *is* what the other aims at. Therefore the relations among parts exist for the sake of the unifying structure, not vice versa. Hence, if the form of this structure is found among the partial associations of [people], much more should it be found in the society of [people] as a totality . . . since the total structure or its form is the greater good. This unifying structure is found in all parts of human society; therefore it is found or should be found in [humankind] as a whole.[18]

As we see, order in the temporal realm is synonymous not only with peace but also with the "right order of society." The ideal goal of human civilization is to realize the potentiality of humanity, and this can only be achieved in a well-ordered universal society. Thus Dante, unlike Aquinas and Augustine, who place this world within a hierarchical system of order in which the supernatural order remains supreme, rejects the view that nature and the state are codependent means for the attainment of a higher order. His main thesis is that we possess the natural right and the intellectual capacity to realize the "blessedness of this life"; our autonomous reason, our "own powers," makes it possible for us to pursue the ends of humanity.[19] The critical distinction that Dante makes is that the *corpus mysticum* is not, as in Aquinas, a complement of nature; rather it too comes directly from God—Christ, the founder of the *corpus mysticum,* expressly stated that "his kingdom is not of this world."[20] Each person has a twofold aim: as a citizen, a this-worldly end; if a Christian, a supernatural *telos,* and these ends are fulfilled in separate orders and are attained by separate means.

Etienne Gilson emphasizes the unique and radical nature of Dante's thesis concerning the twofold nature of human nature. As he says,

> the most remarkable thing about Dante's attitude is that he understood, with a profundity of thought for which he must be commended, that *one cannot entirely withdraw the temporal world from the jurisdiction of the spiritual world without entirely withdrawing philosophy from the jurisdiction of theology.* It is because he clearly saw this fact and plainly indicated it that Dante occupies a cardinal position in the history of medieval political philosophy. For after all, if philosophic reason, by which the Emperor is guided, were to remain in the smallest degree subject to the authority of the theologians, the Pope would through their agency recover the authority over the Emperor which it is desired to take from him. By the very fact that he controlled reason, he would control the will that is guided by reason. Thus, the separation of Church and Empire necessarily presupposes the separation of theology and philosophy, and that is why, just as he split mediaeval Christendom into two camps, Dante also completely shatters the unity of Christian wisdom, the unifying principle and the bond of Christendom. In each of these vital matters this al-

leged Thomist struck a mortal blow at the doctrine of St. Thomas Aquinas [emphasis in original].[21]

Dante's purpose was not, as it was with Aquinas, to separate theology from philosophy in order to reconcile and unite them. And thus even though Dante's utopian universe remains Christian, "it is so after his own fashion, and it does not admit of identification with any other known type of mediaeval Christian universe. Grace does not absorb nature, as in Roger Bacon, for example; it does not penetrate the inner nature, as in St. Thomas Aquinas; it is not eliminated to the advantage of nature, as in Averroes; [and] it does not oppose nature, as in the Latin Averroists of the type of Siger of Brabant."[22]

However, we find that despite the radical cast of Dante's proposition about humanity's twofold nature and purpose it nonetheless remains that for Dante the temporal and supertemporal realms are still linked, albeit tangentially, and the supertemporal realm is still viewed as the superior one. In the last chapter of the *Monarchia* Dante reiterates the twofold nature of human nature—"twofold are the ends which unerring Providence has ordained for [humankind]"—and he repeats that "it is now clear that the authority of temporal world-government must come directly, without intermediary, from the universal Fount of authority." But he also adds a significant qualification that seriously weakens his notion of a dualism of orders:

> And inasmuch as the condition of our globe depends on the order inherent in the revolving heavens, it is needful to have the useful teachings of liberty and peace adapted to times and places by one supervisor, to whom the total state of the heavens is visible at once; and He alone is such a being who in his providence sees to it that all things are ordered as he himself has preordained. If this be the case, God alone elects, he alone establishes governments, for he has none above him. . . . Caesar therefore owes to Peter the piety which a first-born son owes to his father. And so, in the light of paternal grace, this government will better enlighten our globe, over which it rules through Him alone who is the ruler of all things spiritual and temporal.[23]

Dante's conception of temporal order is, as with previous thinkers, still associated with the idea that its origin is traceable to God. As Marjorie Reeves has remarked, "in spite of his efforts to create an absolute division between the two, Dante at the last opens a door through which the ecclesiastics could once more invade the political territory."[24]

In Marsilius of Padua's *Defensor Pacis* we find a much stronger emphasis on the proposition that the temporal world is fully autonomous. Although there are some close parallels between the two thinkers, the ideas proposed by Marsilius in the *Defensor Pacis* differ in critical ways from those expressed by Dante in *De Monarchia*. Marsilius in the *Defensor Pacis* presents three main propositions: first, that the state is the product of reason and that its purpose is to make possible the "sufficient life"; second, that political authority is necessary in order to "moderate" and "proportion" human actions; and third, that the sole source of legitimate political power is the "will and consent" of the people. As we shall see, Marsilius departs radically from the traditional way of thinking which sees the order of the temporal world as linked with supertemporal order, and the state as having its origin in divine providence.

For Marsilius, as for Aquinas and Dante, human beings are by nature social and political animals, and it is, therefore, according to nature that people form associations. In his words, human beings are "born composed of contrary elements . . . and born bare and unprotected:

> As a consequence, [we] need arts of diverse genera and species to avoid the afore-mentioned harms. But since these arts can be exercised only by a large number of [people], and can be had only through their association with one another, [people] had to assemble together in order to attain what was beneficial through these arts and to avoid what was harmful. But since among [human beings] thus assembled there arise disputes and quarrels which, if not regulated by a norm of justice, would cause [people] to fight and separate and thus finally would bring about the destruction of the state, there had to be established in this association a standard of justice and a guardian or maker thereof.[25]

Again, society and politics are a necessity of nature; the state is the product of human reason and is the most perfect association human beings can form: "The things which are necessary for living and for living well were brought to full development by reason and experience, and there was established the perfect community, called the state."[26]

Like Aristotle, Marsilius sees the state as an end in itself and as existing in order that we may achieve the good life (which he calls the "sufficient life"). People are "assembled for the sake of the sufficient life, being able to seek out for themselves the necessaries enumerated above, and exchanging them with one another. This assemblage, thus perfect and having the limit of self-sufficiency, is called the state."[27] And since "diverse things are necessary to [people] who desire a sufficient life, things which cannot be supplied by [those] of one order or office, there had to be diverse orders or offices of [those] in this association."[28] To live and live well involves "moderating and proportioning" our actions and passions. The state is thus a "perfect community" whose functional "parts" are collectively able to provide for all of our human needs. Using Aristotle's discussion in the *Politics* as a starting-point, Marsilius says:

> Let us assume with Aristotle in his *Politics* . . . that the state is like an animate nature or animal. For just as an animal well disposed in accordance with nature is composed of certain proportioned parts ordered to one another and communicating their functions mutually and for the whole, so too the state is constituted of certain such parts when it is well disposed and established in accordance with reason. The relation, therefore, of the state and its parts to tranquillity will be seen to be similar to the relation of the animal and its parts to health. The trustworthiness of this inference we can accept from what all [people] comprehend about each of these relations. For they think that health is the best disposition of an animal in accordance with nature, and likewise that tranquillity is the best disposition of a state established in accordance with reason. Health, moreover, as the more experienced physicists describe it, is the good disposition of the animal whereby each of its parts can perfectly perform the operations belonging to its

nature; according to which analogy tranquillity will be the good disposition of the city or state whereby each of its parts will be able perfectly to perform the operations belonging to it in accordance with reason and its establishment.[29]

Since we do not receive "entirely perfect from nature the means whereby these proportions are fulfilled," it is necessary to use reason in order to "effect and preserve" the proper proportioning of our actions.[30] The parts of the state are established in accordance with reason and experience, and their purpose is to ensure the tranquillity of the well-ordered community. Thus, whereas Dante viewed the state, or temporal order, within the context of a dualism of orders, Marsilius sees it in the image of a living organism. As Reeves puts it:

> Marsiglio places politics within a biological context and starts his analysis from instinctive desires. Where Dante sees the meaning of politics in terms of a progression towards our true nature, which is our end, Marsiglio sees it as a series of consequences following from a biological drive which is our predetermined beginning. His political doctrines follow with a kind of inevitability which is new because it derives from beginnings, not ends. Here the contrast between the two thinkers is reinforced by the striking difference of the analogies they use: whereas Marsiglio, envisaging his perfect state, thinks of the healthy animal organism, Dante, seeking for a symbol of ideal political harmony, finds it in the divinely-ordered and immovable hierarchy of the cosmos.[31]

Several critics have commented on the fact that throughout the *Defensor Pacis* Marsilius is preoccupied by the threat of the destruction of the state and by the essential need to maintain peace to prevent the perpetual conflict that is characteristic of the precommunal condition of humankind.[32] "In even the most highly advanced society," according to Marsilius, "the threat of strife leading to disintegration lingers barely beneath the surface."[33] With Augustine and Dante, as we have seen, one of the major purposes of the state is to maintain peace so that people may have the conditions they need to enable them to focus on a world that transcends historical time, on the one hand, or to strive to achieve the actualization of their full potential in the temporal world, on the other. To Marsilius the sole purpose of peace, or tranquillity, is to bring about cooperation among people in the pursuit of their common interests and benefits. We have observed that for Marsilius tranquillity means "the good disposition of the city or state, whereby each of its parts can perform the functions appropriate to it in accordance with reason and its establishment." However, a fundamental characteristic of those who live in community is a tendency to engage in "disputes and quarrels." Tranquillity is the essential ingredient necessary to bring about and maintain the "mutual association of the citizens, their intercommunication of their functions with one another, their mutual aid and assistance, and in general the power, unimpeded from without, of exercising their proper and common functions, and also the participation in common benefits and burdens according to the measure appropriate to each."[34] The regulation of communal relationships required for the achievement of the "sufficient life" can only be established in that community where "civil peace or tranquillity exists and is preserved, and whereby the opposed strife arises and is checked and destroyed."[35] Peace is not viewed in cosmological terms nor is it seen as an innate need of the human condition; on the contrary, it is simply a necessary requirement to restore and maintain peaceful cooperation among the members of the community and the proper interrelationship among the various parts of the state.

We have seen that for Aquinas and Dante the temporal world, although a product of nature and human reason, is still linked with an otherworldly divine realm; consequently, this world, for Aquinas, requires perfection by grace, and for Dante, is enhanced by "the light of grace." For Marsilius, in contrast, the temporal world is sufficiently justified by nature and requires no "perfecting" by divine grace. In other words, there is no integration of temporal order and divine order in Marsilius's thought.[36] In the *Defensor Pacis* the concept of order is not used in the cosmological sense that we find in Plato and in Augustine, philosophers who interpreted the phenomenal world as either governed or guided by divine supernatural order. On the contrary, when Marsilius uses the term *order* he always refers to the way in which people relate to each other according to some kind of temporal association or membership.[37] In brief, the notion of order in the

Defensor Pacis refers solely to the "order of the parts of the state in relation to one another." As Marsilius says,

> From what we have said, it can be sufficiently clear what is the order of the parts of the state in relation to one another. For all the other parts are ordered by and toward the ruler as the first of all the parts for the status of the present world. For in the civil community that part is first which has to establish, determine, and conserve the others in and for the status of the present world or the civil end. But such is the part which rules in accordance with human law, as we have already concluded by probable and demonstrative reasoning. Therefore, it is the first of all the parts of the state, and the others are ordered to it.[38]

In the Marsilian concept of order we find no dualism of orders; rather there is only one order and that is the order of the arrangement of things in the temporal world. Order consists not in our relation to an ideal otherworldly realm but in the relationship between the individual and the various parts of the state. From Marsilius's point of view order has to do solely with the idea of that harmonious interrelation whereby each part of the state "can perfectly perform the operations belonging to it in accordance with reason and its establishment." As Alan Gewirth points out, "it is noteworthy that Marsilius does not use the concept of order in that cosmological and moral sense in which the medieval tradition, from Augustine on, interpreted the entire world and all its parts as an order governed by God."[39] In abandoning the concept of cosmological order as the sustaining principle in all orders, and by insisting that the temporal order is not linked to a transcendent order, Marsilius emphasizes the notion of the total autonomy and self-sufficiency of the political order and, concurrently, the idea that the ultimate aim of human acts is the achievement of the "sufficient" life in this world. The distance between this doctrine and that of Augustine is obvious; for Augustine the state is nothing more than a remedial instrument, for Marsilius it is an end in itself.

To summarize, then, we have seen that the common outlook that informed the medieval attitude toward the natural order was that it had been assigned an inferior and subordinate status within a hierarchical system of divine cosmological order. Aquinas was the first medieval thinker to challenge seriously the Augustinian notion of the natural order as a consequence of sin and the notion of the state as a remedial instrument provided by God for human salvation. Aquinas argues that the natural order operates on its own principles and that the state is founded upon human nature itself. The demarcation Aquinas made between faith and reason, and the distinction he drew between the natural order and the supernatural order, were a clear departure in thought from the traditional medieval view of the relationship between this world and a supreme supernatural world, and the connection between knowledge and spiritual illumination. In Aquinas, although there always remains a link between the two realms of being and between two modes of comprehension, the temporal world and reason have, nevertheless, their own domain and their own legitimate purpose. Aquinas's view is that faith deals with those divine truths that cannot be comprehended by reason, and reason deals with human truths. Unlike Augustine, who regards truth as inseparable from revelation and as entirely dependent upon grace, Aquinas sees the sensible world, or nature, as the source of all rational knowledge. Reason, in other words, begins with the senses and belongs to the phenomenal rather than the supernatural realm; human knowledge, therefore, can be known through natural phenomena and experience. Human nature makes it possible for human beings to comprehend rational knowledge without the aid of divine grace; divine grace added to natural knowledge enables us to know also the truths of revelation. In thus drawing a distinction between faith and reason, Aquinas effected a beginning of a revolution of thought that later gave rise, as we have seen, to the proposition that reason could stand in its own right, wholly independent of faith.

Yet even though Aquinas's interpretation of the order of the universe and of human nature was a primary influence on the emergence of the doctrine of truth as twofold, his concept of theocentric order, like Augustine's, served, finally, to glorify the supernatural and the divine. It is in Dante and Marsilius that we find a much more complete isolation of the temporal world from the supernatural realm and a far greater separation of the truths of faith from the truths of reason. Both *De Monarchia* and the *Defensor Pacis* emphasize a fundamental belief in the integrity of human reason, in the value of the temporal realm, and in the right of humankind to pursue the good life in this world. Unlike Dante's argument that there are two ends for humankind, and that we pursue both ends by means of the truths of reason (truths aided by divine grace), in Marsilius's view the truths of reason and faith are fully separated from each other. Marsilius denies the relevance of eternal ends to our experience in the temporal world and focuses in the *Defensor Pacis* only on our this-worldly end. In contrast to Dante's explanation concerning the two ends of humankind, "to Marsiglio the horizon of this life cuts the two ends sharply apart. The civic end is severed at that point, but in this life it is absolute. The eternal end is certainly to be recognized here as a kind of invisible line running through the consciences of individuals . . . but it does not exist here in external acts, for it has no coercive force: its realm is the next world."[40] In Marsilius we see the end of the attempt to explain the relationship between different kinds of truth and, in turn, between temporal and eternal order. Marsilius informs us that he is not going to discuss the governance and design of this world by any agency other than the human will—"I shall discuss the establishment of only those laws and governments which emerge immediately from the decision of the human mind."[41]

But Marsilius still retained traces of the general medieval attitude in his view of the temporal world and, in his discussion on the relationship between church and state, that is, between religion and politics, he argues that while the two ends of humanity are sharply separated and do not impinge upon each other, "political power derives ultimately from God and serves a divine function."[42] In brief, for Marsilius the people and their elected government have been appointed by God to have "authority" over all things in the temporal world.

By the time of the humanistic movement of the fifteenth and sixteenth centuries, the medieval way of interpreting the world had disappeared, and a different manner of perceiving it emerged. The main feature of the change that occurred was a shift in perspective from an otherworldly to a this-worldly orientation. This shift in outlook resulted in a new view of the relationship between the individual and nature and between the individual and the state. In its broad outlines, Renaissance humanism is characterized by a confidence in nature—a belief in the certainty of reason and in the human capacity to control the natural world. Fifteenth- and sixteenth-century thinkers, while they did not abandon their belief that a divine meaning underlay the universe, gave up completely the traditional notion of order as being of divine origin with the natural order subservient to the supernatural order. The attitude toward order in the fifteenth and sixteenth centuries, as we shall see in the next chapter, is one that focuses on the kind of order that "ought" to prevail in relations between and among people and, concomitantly, the kind of ordering relationship that should exist in the social and political institutions that are created by people who live in community. This new notion of order, along with the concept of truth as twofold, led, not surprisingly, to a radically new vision of the world and of the individual's place in it; it led also to the appearance in the sixteenth century of the first modern utopia— Thomas More's *Utopia*.

Chapter 4

Reshaping Order: Thomas More's *Utopia*

*I*t is typical to study Thomas More's *Utopia* for its commentary on the social ills of sixteenth-century England, its representation of a community where all people are created equal, or its tightly structured social institutions that serve to control all facets of human activity.[1] In this chapter I want to explore More's meaning in the *Utopia* through a study of the concept of order that he sets forth in that work. From this perspective, it can be argued that a primary aim of the whole book was to offer an alternative explanation of the relation between human beings and order in the temporal realm. Given the change in thought that had occurred by the time of the Renaissance, we would perhaps expect to find that More's views on order would differ somewhat from those of his predecessors. But what is most significant, as we shall see, is that in the *Utopia* More departs not only from the predominant medieval idea that the natural order is defined according to a theory of divine order, but also from the prevailing classical notion that the natural order is the result of our understanding of a supertemporal realm of order, a transcendent realm of order which is the source of order in the phenomenal world. Before turning to an examination of the *Utopia*, a brief review of the main characteristics of the general attitude toward the concept of order in earlier periods will enable us to more fully understand the significant difference in the point of view found in More's thought.

The discussion in the previous chapters has shown us that, through the fourteenth century, the subject matter of concepts of order consisted in large measure of the attempt to render the natural order compatible with the requirements of cosmological order. Sometimes, as with the Stoics and Augustine, the vision of the order of the universe has produced a conceptualization that devalues the natural order, while at other times, as with Plato, the vision of cosmic order has served to exalt the natural order. Yet although the overall characteristic of the history of concepts of order is the attempt to explain a relationship between two realms of being—the natural and the supernatural—a central focus of this mode of thought is, as we have also seen, a dialogue on the theme of the relationship between humankind and the natural order; that is, between the individual and nature. And this aspect of the topic has involved a number of interrelated considerations. The discussion has turned on basic beliefs about the nature of human nature, about the origins of society and of the state, about the idea of membership, and about the natural order.

I mentioned in chapter 1 that in the period prior to the development of Greek thought, philosophers regarded humankind and society as integral parts of nature—the individual was part of society, society was part of nature, and the divine was immanent in both humankind and nature.[2] From this point of view, the realm of nature and the realm of human beings are not distinguished; rather, natural phenomena are conceived in terms of human experience. And since human beings are not separate from nature, reason does not operate autonomously; hence there can be no rational explanation of human experience or of natural phenomena. For the ancients, then, the explanation of both natural and social events took the form not of detached intellectual explanation but of imaginative speculation. And since ideas about society were undifferentiated from consideration of other phenomena, active thought and discussion about political and social questions as an isolated form of speculation was unknown. There was, in other words, no concept of the state as an entity separate from the cosmos; rather, the relationship among people was explained in terms of the concept of shared membership in a cosmic society that encompassed all of creation.

In Greek thought this attitude toward nature underwent deep change.[3] As we have seen in our discussion of Plato's ideas, the Greeks held that the universe is an intelligible whole made up of distinct but interrelated parts, and that a single rational order underlies all natural phenomena. Within this overall scheme, the Greeks saw nature as independent of human nature, and as something comprehensible to human intellect. The link between nature and human nature in Greek thought is not the idea that nature is immanent in society but rather that nature and humanity are governed by the same laws, a dynamic principle active throughout the universe. And it is reason which makes it possible for us to analyze and come to understand those laws that govern both the cosmos and humankind. The problem of understanding nature is thus transferred from the sphere of imaginative mythopoeic speculation to the realm of intellectual discourse. Not unexpectedly, this new outlook led to a quite different explanation of the origins of society. Society now is seen not as an integral part of nature and the result of the will of the gods but as independent of the cosmos and as the product of human nature. Thus when the Greeks speak of society they are in truth speaking of that which is natural to the sum of human experience—the unity which constitutes the *polis* is part of the unity that obtains in human beings and in the universe.[4] The state then is the consequence of human nature. For Plato it has its origins in human need and is the outcome of mutual necessity; for Aristotle it is the product of our natural end or purpose, the fulfillment of our "being." For both thinkers the state is, finally, according to human nature and, therefore, natural.[5] The distinction between society and state that we find in the theories of later thinkers is alien to classical thought; the state does not, in the Greek view, stand in contradistinction to society.

In contrast, the concept of the individual as fundamentally "social," as we have already seen, forms the basis of Stoic doctrine. Unlike Plato and Aristotle, who believe that we share membership in a single natural society-state, the Stoics propose that we share dual membership: on the one hand, we are members of a natural universal society, and on the other we are members of a conventional temporal state. The Stoic doctrine of dual membership led to a sharp distinction between the concepts of society and state—the origin of the universal society is the immanent reason or *logos* that pervades the universe and which unites all humankind; the state is the consequence of a "primitive catastrophe"[6] brought on by our having passed from the natural state of innocence and happiness to the unnatural state of corruption and vice. From this perspective, the function of the state is not, as other Greek thinkers had seen it, to enable us to "grow" to perfection, but rather to constrain the evil tendencies of human nature.[7]

The Stoic reinterpretation of nature thus produced a theory that substituted for the Greek notion of membership in a single natural *polis* the concept of dual membership—one natural, the other conventional. The similarity between these ideas and Augustinian doctrine is obvious. For Augustine, too, human beings are by nature social and they share membership in either one or the other of two universal societies—the *civitas Dei* or the *civitas terrena*. Emphasizing the idea that human beings are "social animals," Augustine's thought turns on the distinction between the natural state of humankind in society before the fall and the actual conditions and circumstances of life in the temporal world. According to Augustine, and the Stoics, in the natural condition of innocence the state was not necessary. But humankind departed from nature and fell into a condition that is against nature; hence, the state is a consequence of our fallen condition. Again, society is natural, the state is conventional. Human beings are by nature social but not political beings—the two universal societies are the result of our sociability; the state is the consequence of a fall from nature and is both a divinely appointed punishment and a remedial instrument provided by God for our possible redemption. Unlike the *polis,* which for Greek thinkers was the only natural form of human community and which had no existence outside the temporal world, for Augustine the only natural membership we share is in a universal society that has its origins not in human nature but in divine providence, and that transcends not only the state but the phenomenal world as well. Augustine, like the Stoics, thus puts forth a theory of the nature of human nature that is committed to the idea of membership in a society that is both superior to and outside of the state.

In contrast to this perspective, Thomas Aquinas, as we saw earlier, believed that human beings and nature, and, in turn, the state, are governed by principles that are according to the natural order. For Aquinas human beings are by nature social and political beings; they are political animals because they are by nature social beings. Human beings fulfill the end of their social and political being through membership in a natural temporal state. If a Christian, however, they are also members of the *corpus mysticum,* and they fulfill the end of their spiritual nature through membership in a supernatural society. Basic to Aquinas's thinking is the notion of two orders of membership, one natural, the other supernatural. As a member of the natural order our natural end is the fulfillment of our rational nature in the temporal state; if a member of the *corpus mysticum* our natural end is, in addition, the fulfillment of our spiritual nature in the heavenly city. Again, there are two orders of membership, but these orders, as Aquinas saw it, are not, as they were for Augustine, mutually exclusive or incompatible. The dichotomy between nature and the supernatural that we find in Augustine is reconciled by Aquinas through the concept of cosmic order as an interrelated and harmonious hierarchy of orders constituted of "natures" that tend toward their own end according to the principles of the order to which they belong. Consequently, our temporal condition is governed by the principles of the natural order, and membership in a political society is according to nature. And since nature has provided us with reason, the state is the culmination of our understanding of the natural order of the universe. At the same time, because we are not born self-sufficient, the state is the product of our natural inclination to form associations in order to achieve the perfection of our earthly needs. Thus whereas the bond of the *corpus mysticum* is faith and divine grace, the bond of the state is reason and mutual necessity. But, finally, although Aquinas's ideas differ from the Augustinian view, it nonetheless remains that for Aquinas also the transpolitical realm of order is still the superior order of membership.[8]

It was in the fourteenth century that the attitude toward the natural order and the origin of the state changed fundamentally. And this change, as I have already mentioned, is directly linked to the emergence of the doctrine of truth as twofold. A mode of thought which proposes that nothing can be rationally demonstrated about revelation while at the same time asserting that the phenomenal world can be fully understood by reason, the concept of truth as twofold gave rise to the renewal of the view of the state as natural and as the product of unaided reason. There is, then, as we saw in the previous chapter, no mention whatsoever in Dante's utopian vision in *De Monarchia* or in Marsilius's *Defensor Pacis* of the idea that human beings share membership in a universal transpolitical society. For Dante and Marsilius, as for many other fourteenth-century thinkers, such a concept is identified with otherworldly interests and with faith and is, therefore, a notion incapable of rational explanation on the one hand,

and not relevant in discussions of the order of this world on the other.

By the time of the Renaissance the acceptance of the notion of truth as twofold resulted in a radical change in attitude in which the emphasis now was on human nature, reason, the law of nature and the natural order without reference to their being predetermined or controlled by a supreme supernatural being. Against the traditional view of human beings and nature as imperfect and as dependent upon divine providence stood a new outlook of humanity and nature as governed entirely by reason and by absolute rather than relative natural law.[9] From this viewpoint, nature is seen as complete in itself and as possessing its own intrinsic perfection, and human beings are regarded as having within themselves the means of attaining fully their own natural end. With this change in attitude toward human nature and the temporal realm, it is not surprising that the quest for order also assumed an entirely different character from the patterns of the past. By the sixteenth century the search for a concept of order became increasingly a study of the state and of a theory of political order. This new notion of order, with its focus on the creation of an ideal state that directs humankind toward the attainment of the good life in this world, informs the most famous of all "well-ordered commonwealths," Thomas More's *Utopia*.

In the *Utopia* More clearly advocates the doctrine of truth as twofold and proceeds to sharply divide the truths of reason from those of revelation. Indeed, in Utopia religion is founded not on revelation at all but on philosophy and natural reason. Thus although they accept the notion of a teleological universe, the Utopians hold that reason, not revelation, affirms religious truths. From this point of view, the truths of religion cannot be in conflict with the truths of nature for both are determined by natural reason without the aid of divine illumination. For More, then, unlike Aquinas, there is a "natural" rather than a "revealed" connection between religious and philosophical truths.[10] Acknowledging, however, that reason falls short of understanding all of the mysteries in nature, the Utopians supplement their rational understanding of natural phenomena by uniting philosophy with "certain principles taken from religion."[11] Like Duns Scotus and Ockham, the Utopians hold that reason leads us to affirm certain fundamental religious truths that are arrived at according to strictly philosophical arguments. Reason thus persuades all Utopians to believe that there is "one supreme being to whom are due both the creation and the providential government of the whole world,"[12] that "the soul is immortal,"[13] and that "after this life rewards are appointed for our virtues and good deeds, punishment for our crimes."[14] Having established these fundamental religious principles, More makes clear that the Utopians do not attempt to adjust rational inquiry to the demands of revelation. To the contrary, they have concluded and are in complete agreement that God is a being "unknown, eternal, immense, inexplicable, [and] far above the reach of the human mind."[15]

The emphasis throughout the *Utopia* is on reason, nature, and the place of human beings in the natural realm. The starting point for More is the idea that we can rely only upon unaided reason for guidance in this world; the only truths the Utopians know are those arrived at through the use of natural reason. In More's view, as it is presented in the *Utopia*, to attempt to understand and explain the natural order and human nature according to supernatural truths is at once unreasonable and against nature. From the point of view of reason, human beings and nature are absolutely natural and absolutely self-sufficient. While their reverence of a supreme being and their belief in immortality may reassure the Utopians of a just reward beyond this life, this otherworldly perspective does not inform their understanding of this world or the nature of human nature. In contrast to previous thinking there is no mention in the *Utopia* of human beings sharing membership in a universal transpolitical society, of two coterminous realms of being, or of a rational *logos* immanent in society and in humanity. On the contrary, in the *Utopia* More proposes that by intellect alone, without appeal to transcendent principles or supernatural authority, and without relying upon nonrational faculties, human beings can understand the phenomenal realm and, possibly, create a rationally ordered intelligible world.

Indeed, from the viewpoint of order, the most striking feature of the *Utopia* is that, unlike the earlier thematic outlook, More does not treat the natural order as part of cosmological order, or the natural order as a subordinate realm in a hierarchical scheme of divine order. Nor is temporal order dependent upon divine mediation or explained according to a concept of an ideal realm of Forms or Ideas. A close reading of the *Utopia* reveals that, unlike his predecessors who argue confidently from the vision of an order that was established and maintained by either a top principle in the universe or by a creator-God, the starting point for More is simply our involvement with this world and the attempt to find order in that world. Thus More does not start out looking for first causes or underlying principles that result in temporal order; rather, he locates order in our involvement in society and he concerns himself with the kind of order that "ought" to prevail in relations between and among people. Ignoring the traditional view that there exists a link between temporal and cosmic order, in the *Utopia* More presents a notion of order that is defined strictly in terms of humanity's relationship to social and political institutions.

More's description of life in Utopia begins in Book II, and it is immediately apparent that he intends to look at order whole[16] and that he plans to propose that order in the temporal realm is solely the product of reason. In a few short opening paragraphs we are suddenly in a new "world," and within two pages we learn that the inhabitants of this world have not only rationally planned their life but even altered their natural environment to fit their needs and desires. Thus although Utopia was not at first an island, the Utopians excavated "fifteen miles on the side where the land was connected with the continent and caused the sea to flow around the land."[17] Having established the background to be used for his discussion of order, More directly proceeds to a description of the order of Utopia's city-states:

> The island contains fifty-four city-states, all spacious and magnificent, identical in language, traditions, customs, and laws. They are similar in layout and everywhere, as far as the nature of the ground permits, similar even in appearance. None of them is separated by less than twenty-four miles from the nearest, but none is so isolated that a person cannot go from it to another in a day's journey on foot.[18]

To give the reader a greater sense of the order that obtains throughout his "ideal" commonwealth—as he says, "the person who knows one of the cities will know them all, since they are exactly alike"[19]—

More's method is to begin with a detailed description of the orderly arrangement of "things"[20] in the city of Amaurotum which, because it is located in the center of the country, is considered the capital city. The following passages, which describe Amaurotum, are typical of More's method throughout the *Utopia* of focusing on specific details whenever he is discussing the orderly arrangement of things in his ideal commonwealth.

> Amaurotum is situated on the gentle slope of a hill and is almost four-square in outline. Its breadth is about two miles starting just below the crest of the hill and running down to the river Anydrus; its length along the river is somewhat more than its breadth.[21]

> The city is surrounded by a high and broad wall with towers and battlements at frequent intervals. A moat, dry but deep and wide and made impassable by thorn hedges, surrounds the fortifications on three sides; on the fourth the river itself takes the place of the moat.

> The streets are well laid out both for traffic and for protection against the winds. . . . The house fronts of the respective blocks are divided by an avenue twenty feet broad. On the rear of the houses, through the whole length of the block, lies a broad garden enclosed on all sides by the backs of the blocks. Every home has not only a door into the street but a back door into the garden.[22]

Next, we see that order in the *Utopia* encompasses not only the physical environment but human activities as well. Hence, on every street in each of the cities there is a spacious hall located at equal distance from each other where 30 families, 15 from each side of the street, are assigned to take their meals in common. Every city is divided into four equal districts, and in the middle of each district there is a market building where commodities are arranged separately. In sum, More's cities are based upon a condition of physical order created by the inhabitants to allow for a close control over the details of everyday life. Thus in Utopia physical order is analogous to and serves as the foundation for the order of social life. Work is strictly organized, and everyone works the prescribed six hours. And all work is performed for the benefit of everyone, not for personal profit. This kind of detailed prescription governing economic arrangements is applied also to education, family, religion, and cultural life. All aspects of social and political life in Utopia are governed by the objective of order. By attending to the close regulation of the activities of the Utopians, it is possible to regularize human behavior and thus to eliminate, as far as possible, disorder.

After his account of the physical conditions of Utopia's city-states, and of the relationship of these physical conditions to the values and interests of the Utopians,[23] More turns to his main theme, the analysis of political order. Following Plato's method of applying the properties of mathematics to a political scheme, similar to the plan described by Plato in the *Laws*,[24] More relies primarily upon numbers to create a system of harmonious political order. The basic social and political unit in Utopia is the family. And each family, or household, is limited to between 10 and 16 adults:

> Since the city consists of households, households as a rule are made up of those related by blood. . . . But that the city neither be depopulated nor grow beyond measure, provision is made that no household shall have fewer than ten or more than sixteen adults; there are six thousand such households in each city, apart from its surrounding territory. Of children under age, of course, no number can be fixed. This limit is easily observed by transferring those who exceed the number in larger families into those that are under the prescribed number. Whenever all the families of a city reach their full quota, the adults in excess of that number help to make up the deficient population of other cities.[25]

Thus to keep the size of each household uniform, children may be moved from one family to another, and when the adults in each family exceed the prescribed number they are shifted from one city to another so as to keep the population of the cities uniform. Each city then has a population of between 60,000 and 96,000 adult citizens. For administrative purposes the cities are divided into four major quarters or districts. Every year 30 families elect an official called a "syphogrant,"[26] and over every 10 syphogrants with their families there is a "tranibor." There are 200 syphogrants in each city, and they constitute a senate which elects the mayor of the city from one of the four candidates nominated by the families in each district.

It is not necessary to give all of the details More provides about the way in which life in Utopia is organized. A few examples will suffice. In addition to his description of the physical order and numerical order that obtain in Utopia, More gives an extended account of how the daily activities of the entire community are integrated into a unified and ordered structure. In their public life the Utopians are summoned at set hours to take their meals in common halls where people are arranged according to age and gender, and where the syphogrant presides at a table which offers a full view of the whole assembly. A similar kind of highly structured behavior is followed by the Utopians in their other main form of common gathering—religious worship. They celebrate holy days on the first and last days of each month, and when they gather in the temple they are seated, as in the common halls where they take their meals, according to sex, age, and position of authority within the family. In brief, in their private and public life the Utopians are governed by a strict timetable and by a structured form of behavior that results in a tightly organized social order.

In More's view, as was noted earlier, order is not a self-sustaining condition. As we have also seen, one of the leading motifs in Western political thought is the idea that order in the temporal realm is dependent upon and sustained by a transcendent realm of order. In direct contrast to this view, More proposes in the *Utopia* that temporal order depends entirely on the constant exercise of political authority. Hence great emphasis is placed on discipline and obedience within the basic political unit in Utopia—the patriarchal family. Again and again, More emphasizes the importance of the patriarchal family as a bedrock of political society, and he underscores its foundational-political function by having the rule of the patriarchal head backed by Utopia's public officials. Thus order in the family is maintained by the authority of parents over children, of husbands over wives, and of the eldest, the patriarch, over the entire household. And just as it is the responsibility of the patriarchal head to maintain order in the family, it is the function of the syphogrants and the tranibors to preserve social order. Through the harmonization they achieve by minutely regulating their conduct, by indoctrinating the people in the basic teachings of their society, and by means of discipline, the Utopians become at once both the product and the creators of order.

While More's method is to present his views on order through a detailed description of the arrangement of life in Utopia, it should be clear that his main interest in the work is not the most effective numerical scheme upon which to base political institutions, nor the most efficient economic system, nor the ideal arrangement of cities. Such matters are important. However, they are subsumed by the major theme that unites the entire work, namely, the subject of order. More, like earlier thinkers, has as his purpose an analysis of the ordering relationship that exists between human beings and their world. And, when we examine the *Utopia* from this perspective, we find that its major significance lies in the particular "kind" of order that gives structure to the whole work. In contrast to customary ways of comprehending order, the focus in More's vision is on our relationship to order defined exclusively in political terms. Like Plato in the *Republic,* for example, and like Aristotle in the *Politics,* More's intention in the *Utopia* is to reintegrate the individual with political order. But unlike Plato and Aristotle, More does not rely upon a supertemporal realm of order to give meaning and purpose to temporal order. For More natural law and political institutions, not divine providence or an ideal realm of Forms and Ideas, are the agencies of stability and order in the temporal realm.

We have seen that historically all concepts of order have been joined with theories about the origin and purpose of the state. And so too are these ideas linked in More's thought. The view in the *Utopia* is that the origin of the state, like the origin of order, is traceable not to first causes in nature nor to divine providence, but only to human reason. This point of view is very different from the generally prevailing theocentric outlook and from the common framework of the classical point of view. Although there are of course significant differences among the views of earlier thinkers, it nonetheless remains that up through the fifteenth century the dominant concepts of people living in community were based upon theories of causal necessity. In the *Republic*,[27] for example, Plato tells us that the state has its origin in human nature and is the outcome of mutual necessity; for Aristotle, since "nature . . . makes nothing in vain," it is the product of our natural end or purpose, the fulfillment of our "being."[28] For both thinkers, the state is the product of our inherent nature. In Augustinian thought, too, human beings are by nature "social beings."[29] For Augustine, however, the state, which is the result of our fall from the natural state of innocence, is both a divinely appointed punishment and a remedial instrument provided by God for our possible redemption.[30] To put it another way, in Augustinian doctrine the state is at once a sort of supplement to divine grace and is remedial in nature and purpose. From this perspective, we see that just as the view of order had been made relative to our temporal condition after the fall, so too, as Walter Ullmann has also observed, had the origin and purpose of the state been adjusted to accommodate our fallen condition.[31] And finally, for Aquinas we are by nature social and political beings; first by nature a social animal, we are foremost by nature a political animal because only in the political community can we achieve well-being *(bene esse)* or the maximum development of our capacities.[32] In Aquinas's view, since nature has provided us with reason, the state is the product of our understanding of the principles which govern us in the temporal realm.

The essence of the Aristotelian, Augustinian, and Thomistic concepts of nature is thus one of beings who act under the impulse of either an internal or an external inclination seeking the end natural to their kind, and finding their place in the order of being according to their telic determination. Consequently, for Aristotle and Aquinas political life in the state is the natural condition for humankind not merely because we in fact do live in society but because our nature achieves its final fulfillment in the state. Similarly for Augustine membership in a transpolitical society is the natural condition for humankind in its fallen state not merely because we are "by nature social beings" but because divine providence has ordained that we fulfill ourselves as a member of either one or the other of two universal societies.[33] According to Augustine, membership in one or the other of two transpolitical societies directs us toward a life beyond historical time and is our "natural" condition; membership in a temporal society results from our fallen condition and the state, in turn, is the result of divine providence. Thus outside of the Augustinian society on the one hand, or the Aristotelian and Thomistic state on the other, we are by nature a being incomplete. In both instances the individual is perceived as reaching full stature in or being shaped by—rather than as shaping—the state or society since the individual is viewed as deficient apart from a political or social entity. In sum, the Aristotelian, Augustinian, and Thomistic explanations of our fulfilling ourselves in the temporal realm rest upon a natural directedness, a teleological preordination, to specific social goals. Similar views, as we saw in the previous chapter, are found in Dante and Marsilius. For Dante, there are two ends that divine providence has ordained for humankind: "the bliss of this life, . . . and the bliss of eternal life."[34] For Marsilius, following Aristotle, human beings are by nature social and political animals and they fulfill their earthly end within "the perfect community, called the state."[35]

In his explanation of the origin of the state More does not start from the point of view of causal necessity. In fact, unlike those works that put forward a philosophical or theological justification for the origin and purpose of the state, More's *Utopia* presents a political system that is embodied in a design for the arrangement of human affairs and is offered as an alternative to traditional systems of social order. Although his Utopians may fulfill themselves in a political community, More does not, as earlier thinkers do, define human beings as by nature political animals; nor does he speak of the state, as Aristotle does, as a "living being."[36] In a word, the state for More is simply explained by itself. It has no meaning or purpose beyond serving as a social mechanism used by people who live in community to arrange the means by which they can best interact with each other. Reflecting the change in thought that occurred with respect to the meaning of the term *nature,* the "law of nature" in More's view is defined in strictly human terms, not, as it had been earlier, according to a theory of nature at large; that is, it is a view of nature based upon the nature of human nature rather than upon the nature of things in the phenomenal world. As Otto Gierke points out, "the intellectual force which finally dissolved the medieval view of the nature of human groups was the Law of Nature. . . . The Law of Nature issued in a natural-law theory of the state; and it was by developing such a theory that it affected the movement of history most powerfully. . . . Unhistorical in the foundations on which it was built, it was directed, in its efforts and its results, not to the purpose of scientific explanation . . . but to that of the exposition and justification of a new future which was to be called into existence."[37] Against the earlier prevailing view of the individual as fulfilled or shaped by the state, then, stands More's notion of the state as shaped by human reason as a means to the realization of a "new future." In brief, for More the state is merely a beneficial social convention, a human contrivance which owes its origin to human thought and the desire to achieve the good life in a rationally ordered world.

Thus in Utopia what impels people to live in community is not a top principle in nature or the directive of divine providence, but simply a recognition of the general common needs of humanity and the knowledge that one's own individual powers are insufficient to fulfill all of these needs. The bond of the state in Utopia is an awareness of the human desire to achieve the good life in this world and to assist others in their pursuit of the same goal. As John Freeman has observed, "in Utopia there is an overriding concern with balancing what is private and one's own with what is the public interest *("publicum rem")*. The communality stressed in Utopia . . . is tempered by an allowance for individuality so long as that individuality does not move persons to further their own advantage to the disadvantage of their neighbors."[38] Toward this end the Utopians' constitution and their laws are, first, in harmony with the "law" of human reason and, second, designed so that each person may attain happiness and, at the same time, aid in achieving the greatest happiness for others. Consequently, they have very few formal laws, and the laws they do have serve to organize society so that people can fit into the social context in a way that enables them to make the best contribution to the achievement of the good life for themselves and for others. And in the *Utopia* the primary means to the attainment of the good life is political order.

Thus, in contrast to the earlier view, the state for More is at once the product of and determined by the light of human reason independent of general philosophical principles and independent of divine grace. And, just as he had disengaged the temporal from the supertemporal order, so too does More dissociate the state from those theories of nature that linked its origin to first causes. Before he could achieve the latter, however, he first had to break the link between a sovereign supertemporal realm of order and an order in the temporal world. Once that was achieved, the result, as we have seen, is that More in the *Utopia* establishes the sovereignty of human beings over order in the temporal realm.

It is clear that the achievement of the *Utopia* lies primarily not in its political views, nor, as some critics suggest, in its natural religion,[39] but rather in its concept of order. The influence of the notion of order on the *Utopia* has not been emphasized in the study of utopianism, although it is stressed in the work itself. From the point of view of order, we find that in the *Utopia* More is less concerned with the expression of a particular political philosophy than with a conceptualization of a world that is designed by human beings, a world that is informed by, and which in turn conforms to, a concept of order defined strictly in human terms. As the inscription above each book indicates, the main theme of the work is "the best order of society." And More views the best order of society as having nothing to do with divinely ordained cosmic order, that is, with the notion of temporal order as a microcosm which must display the same principles of order prevalent in creation as a whole. On the contrary, for More order in the temporal realm is the product of human reason alone, and it is sustained by those political institutions created by reasonable people who strive to make life within a worldly framework as orderly as possible.

The shift in focus that we find in the *Utopia*, from the viewpoint of order, can be summarized as follows. It was a change from a cosmic vision of order to a temporal vision of order; from a notion of supertemporal order that orients humanity in dependence upon a transcendental model of order to a natural order that orients us to a dependence upon political order; from an order that directs humankind to a *telos* beyond time to an order that directs us to an end in this world; from an order imposed on the world to an order created by human beings. In short, the *Utopia* presents a radically different vision of order, a view of order that focuses solely on the idea of order in the temporal realm, a political order that is independent of any "otherworldly" realm of order. The search for a fresh beginning in understanding this world and our relationship to it is what preoccupied More in the *Utopia,* and for More, the first step in that process was to disengage the temporal realm from cosmic and divine order and to substitute in its place a vision of a basic human mode of ordering, an order subject to human control and one that can be brought about through the use of human reason alone. This fundamental transformation in thought evolved, as we shall see in our study of Francis Bacon's *New Atlantis,* into the notion that order is progressive and continually redefined as new knowledge is acquired about the nature of human nature and about the nature of the phenomenal world.

Chapter 5

Order and Progress: Bacon's *New Atlantis*

We have seen how notions of the state and perspectives on human reason changed as the attitude toward order changed from that of a cosmic universal order to a temporal order that is the result of human reason alone unaided by divine grace. In the preceding chapters I have attempted to show the integral relationship that we find among a number of basic ideas in various historical approaches to defining the concept of order; specifically, the correlation between order and such subjects as human reason, faith, truth, first causes in nature and in human nature, and the origin and purpose of the state. As we saw, it is difficult to miss the links between cosmology, divine providence, and the temporal world in the history of the idea of order and, in turn, of utopian speculation. And the persistent view of an affinity between temporal and supernatural order resulted, as we have seen, from the deep conviction that order in the natural world mirrored the order of the cosmos. In this chapter I wish to focus on the distance between these earlier views and Francis Bacon's outlook on the same issues, a point of view, as we shall see, that inevitably resulted in his dramatically different utopian vision in the *New Atlantis*.

In chapter 4, I stressed that the most distinctive feature of the *Utopia* is its emphasis on order in the temporal world independent of a supernatural realm of order and, concomitantly, its insistence on the idea that temporal order is the product of human reason alone, and, consequently, subject to human rather than divine control. Yet More still retained strong traces of the traditional outlook. His vision of order, for example, while it does not attempt to harmonize the total universe, as do the Platonic and Augustinian concepts of order, is nevertheless a perfect and total order within which the activities of people are blended into an harmonious whole. It is, in brief, an order that is comprehensive, tightly structured, stable, and static. And, as for Plato and Augustine, for More too the function of order is to direct humankind toward a clearly defined and specific *telos*. That More did not make a real break with traditional modes of thought is also seen in the fact that he offers no new explanation of our relation or interaction with nature. As we have seen, in More nature refers solely to that which is natural according to human nature. There is no mention in the *Utopia* of a relationship between human beings and the physical world or of a natural law which governs the general scheme of things in the phenomenal world.[1] In sum, although the focus shifts dramatically in the *Utopia* from an otherworldly to a this-worldly orientation, the work in many respects looks back to classical and medieval ways of thinking.

Bacon's *New Atlantis,* as we shall see, departs in substantial ways not only from More's *Utopia* but from medieval and classical patterns of reasoning generally. To appreciate fully the extent to which Bacon challenges traditional approaches, it is necessary to look initially at some of the major ideas that form the basis of his overall "project of progress," a project that gave rise to the expression of an original future-oriented utopian vision. Bacon's theory of knowledge is well known. Rejecting the Aristotelian method of abstract speculation, with its emphasis on the deduction of particular statements from more general statements, Bacon's focus is on an investigation and interpretation of the particulars of nature. Against the traditional approach of arriving at truth deductively through the use of syllogistic forms, Bacon sets the principle of inductive logic. True knowledge derives not from metaphysical speculation, but from the discovery of the actual nature of things.[2] Bacon thus substitutes for the conceptual and theoretic method of Aristotle and the scholastics the analytical and experiential method. The means to knowledge is the investigation of nature; the method is the application of inductive reasoning to the data of experience. From this point of view, experience is the indispensable element in the verification of truth. The inductive method and experience, Bacon argues, are the surest means of determining the true nature of reality on the one hand, and of advancing knowledge on the other.

Bacon's theory of knowledge also includes a reformulation of the doctrine of truth as twofold, so that it can accommodate "scientific" truths. Again and again, Bacon insists on the separation of the spheres of reason and faith. Like Duns Scotus and More, Bacon holds that truth is twofold: there is truth of faith, and there is truth of reason. But the distinction Bacon draws between natural and supernatural truths is closer to Duns Scotus's view than to that of More. We have seen that in More's view reason cannot confirm revelation. Yet he still proposes that natural reason can affirm, albeit by persuasion and not by demonstration, three fundamental religious beliefs: the existence of God, the immortality of the soul, and human free will. Having established the dual nature of truth, More nonetheless goes on to suggest that it is possible for natural reason to discover some truths about God and about our place in the universe. Thus while faith cannot confirm natural truths, reason is capable of verifying supernatural truths. Against this view, as we have seen, is Duns Scotus's doctrine that matters concerning divine providence are not a subject of reason, but of faith alone; reason cannot, even through persuasion, confirm supernatural truths. Reason and faith are two distinctly different modes of comprehension and they do not inform one another. The point of departure for Duns Scotus is his notion of reason as a limited faculty. And it is precisely because reason is limited that it is incapable of comprehending, much less explaining, supernatural truths.

Bacon too views reason as a limited faculty.[3] Like Duns Scotus, he argues that the truths known by reason cannot transcend the phenomenal world. Thus the "scientific" investigation of nature affirms nothing about supernatural truths. In Bacon's words, if we "shall think by view and inquiry into these sensible and material things to attain that light whereby we may reveal the nature or will of God, then indeed we are spoiled by vain philosophy: for the contemplation of God's creatures and works produceth (having regard to the works and creatures themselves) knowledge; but having regard to God, no perfect knowledge, but wonder."[4] Bacon insists that divine providence does not reveal itself though nature or reason: "Out of the contemplation of nature and elements of human knowledge to induce any conclusion of reason or even any strong persuasion concerning the mysteries of faith, or to inspect and sift them too curiously and search out the manner of the mystery, is not safe. 'Give unto faith the things which are faith's.'"[5] The contemplation of nature has for its end knowledge; but this knowledge is restricted to an understanding of the natural world. Bacon is adamant. Supernatural truths are accepted on faith; they are not revealed by nature or known by reason.[6] To study theology we must "step out of the bark of human reason and enter into the ship of the Church, which is only able by the divine compass to rightly direct its course. Neither will the stars of philosophy, which have hitherto so nobly shone upon us, any longer supply their light." In a word, things human and divine cannot be mingled: "Wherefore we conclude that sacred theology ought to be derived from the world and oracles of God, and not from the light of nature, or the dictates of reason. For it is written, 'the heavens declare the glory of God,' but it is nowhere written, 'the heavens declare the will of God.'"[7] While it is legitimate to exercise reason on the data of revelation in order to try to understand them, we have no grounds on which to expect that revelation will be "agreeable to our reason." Indeed, since reason is limited we should expect to ascribe to revealed truths conclusions that are distorted precisely because they have been made to conform with human understanding. Bacon acknowledges natural theology but its scope is strictly limited. As he puts it in *The Advancement of Learning:* "The bounds of this knowledge, truly drawn, are that it suffices to refute atheism, . . . but not to establish religion."[8] For Bacon there can be no argument from reason to supernatural truths, not even "persuasion concerning the mysteries of faith."

The difference between Bacon and More in their views on natural theology, and on the division of truth into two parts, results to a large extent from the change in the meaning of "reason." By the seventeenth century, the term had come to be used in a new sense: "The old 'reason' that was so much more than merely rational—that was the total mind operating upon a complex and fully representative human experience—vanished along with the organic universe. . . . 'Reason' was exalted; but 'reason' meant only those mental operations that the mathematician and the scientist employed."[9] We have seen that Bacon rejected the syllogistic logic of Aristotle and the scholastics because it relied too much on the earlier, more comprehensive reason. Against this approach to knowledge is Bacon's view that reason must be tied to the observed particulars of nature.

As Stephen Collins points out, "our reasoning faculty had to be framed, shaped, and fed with correct information about the world. Bacon's 'reason' in no way resembled 'right reason' whose innate character reflected and participated in nature's order."[10] For Bacon the faculty of reason enables us to understand the phenomenal world; it does not enable us to affirm metaphysical truths. Bacon's purpose in assigning to reason "the things of reason, and to faith the things of faith," was to establish the independence of science from theology.[11] Only by so doing could knowledge be advanced and, concomitantly, the estate of humankind improved. As he puts it in the *New Atlantis:* "The end of our Foundation is the knowledge of causes and secret motions of things, and the enlarging of the bounds of human empire, to the effecting of all things possible."[12]

Bacon's attitude as expressed in Aphorism XXXVI in the *Novum Organum* represents his typical feeling about all areas of thought—people "must force themselves for awhile to lay their notions by and begin to familiarize themselves with facts."[13] For Bacon it is not only in the study of nature but in all departments of knowledge that preconceptions must be set aside; thought must "begin anew from the very foundations, unless we would revolve for ever in a circle with mean and contemptible progress."[14] Bacon's principal concern in the *New Atlantis,* like More's in the *Utopia,* is not to investigate how God works but to study the relation of humankind to the natural order. But unlike More, Bacon concerns himself not with an interpretation of the "right order" of society but with an investigation of the parts of nature. More, as we have seen, was interested in describing how the good life could be achieved through a smoothly functioning system of political order; Bacon's interest, in contrast, is in describing how the good life can be achieved through the advancement of knowledge based upon a new way of examining the things and events of the material world. The fundamental view shared by Bacon and More is that both were committed, to use Bacon's phrase, to the "relief of our estate." More believed that the means to that end is through political institutions; Bacon, on the other hand, held that the way lies in seeking empirical knowledge. Accordingly, in the *Utopia* we are given details about the proper ordering of political institutions; in the *New Atlantis* Bacon describes such institutions only as they further the acquisition and application of natural knowledge.

As we have seen in earlier chapters, theories of the state have traditionally been joined with concepts about nature in general and about the nature of human nature in particular. This point of view is found in all the notions of the state that we have studied, including More's. It has been the case with Aristotle in his view of human beings as by nature "political animals," with Augustine in his theory that we are by nature "social beings," and with Aquinas in his conception that we are by nature "social and political beings." In all of these concepts the state is viewed as the consequence of our predetermined nature; hence, the state is itself according to nature. Although in More the idea of attributing the origin of the state to a law of nature which governs all phenomena in the natural order is abandoned, the state is nonetheless still viewed as the product of natural law. The departure in More's thought lies in his use of the term *nature*. Unlike his predecessors, More defines nature strictly in terms of human nature. From this point of view, the state is natural not according to first causes in nature, but according to the laws of human nature. Thus while More rejects the notion of the state as the consequence of first causes active throughout the universe, the state is, nonetheless, the result of innate human impulses. It is, as he says, the product of that "fellowship created by nature" that results in our natural inclination to help others. Like Plato, More sees the state as having its origins in human need and as the outcome of mutual dependence; unlike Plato, he views the state as the consequence not of causal necessity but, rather, of our rational nature. Reason directs us toward an awareness of "that fellowship created by nature" and, concomitantly, of the need to live in community in order to fulfill all of our needs.

When we turn to the *New Atlantis,* we notice immediately that Bacon's preoccupation is not with first causes—as Collins puts it, "he neither sought nor celebrated first causes"[15]—or the "right order of society," but, as Bacon himself tells us, with a "description of a college instituted for the interpreting of nature and the producing of great and marvelous works for the benefit of humankind."[16] The text opens with the story of a group of sailors who have been caught in a storm and end up on the island of New Atlantis. We hear about the reception they receive from the Bensalemites and learn some of the familial and religious rituals practiced by the "strange inhabitants" of the island. However, beyond an introductory observation that the people in Bensalem adhere to a natural theology, a statement about the family as the unit upon which society is built,[17] and a glance at the functions of some of the state officials, Bacon devotes little attention to a discussion of the social and political institutions by which the citizens of Bensalem are governed. There is, on the other hand, an extended treatment of the function and purpose of Salomon's House, or, the College of the Six Days Works. As the story unfolds, it becomes clear that New Atlantis is a society that has benefited from the elaborate scientific investigations conducted at Salomon's House, the college established by the Bensalemites for the scientific conquest of nature. The fundamental characteristic of the College of the Six Days Works is that it is dedicated to the systematic study of all natural phenomena; the inhabitants of Salomon's House devote themselves to inquiring into the secrets of nature, into the true "causes and secret motions of things." Accordingly, Bacon gives a lengthy list of the resources available to the members of Salomon's House, the instruments and methods they use, the specific kinds of observations and experiments they are conducting, and their scientific achievements. We learn that all knowledge in Bensalem is derived from an exact observation of natural phenomena, and from an inductive interpretation of the facts of nature. And the end of such knowledge is to expand the empire of human beings over things, to enable us to understand nature and to control it to our own advantage. In Bensalem, as Bacon puts it elsewhere, the true "goal of the sciences is none other than this: that human life be endowed with new discoveries and powers"[18] for the benefit and use of life. Charles Whitney offers a much more skeptical view of the aims of Bacon's utopian vision. As he puts it,

> the New Atlantis is much less a narration of events than it is a narration of procedures, culminating in that of Salomon's House's scientific procedures. . . . At its worst the Baconian search for truth is a furious, compulsive, and ascetic 'ritual' . . . of life-negation. Bacon's utopia and the community of truth-seeking intellectuals at its core thus represent the blind or the secret will to domination and control that ideologies of both reform and revolution can harbor. At its best, Bacon's utopia

represents an affirmative and healing ritual of life that attempts to encompass both reformative and revolutionary possibilities for human realization.[19]

For our purposes, it is impossible not to notice that the *New Atlantis,* unlike earlier conceptions of ideal commonwealths, offers no theory of the state. Although Bacon suggests that the family is the basic political unit in Bensalem, and that marriage is a political as well as a private contract, the *New Atlantis* lacks a complete description of an integrated political order. The state is referred to ("The state will defray you all the time you stay."[20]), a few officials are identified ("I am by office governor of this House of Strangers."[21]), and some public authority is clearly assigned ("The governor assisteth, to the end to put in execution by his public authority the decrees and orders of the Tirsan."[22]), but there is no political world in the *New Atlantis.* Perhaps the most striking evidence of Bacon's lack of concern with the arrangement of social institutions is seen in the fact that private citizens in Bensalem play no political role; although we are told that their lives are regulated by the state, there is no discussion of how the citizen fits into a scheme of government. The only political establishment that Bacon discusses in detail is Salomon's House. This is a community with a strict distribution of labor and of responsibility. There are 36 Fellows who make all decisions that affect the relief of humanity's estate. The most important power the Fellows have is the power to determine which discoveries shall be given to the state and which shall be held back: "We take all an oath of secrecy for the concealing of those [inventions] which we think fit to keep secret, though some of those we do reveal sometimes to the state, and some not."[23] It is significant that the power of the only political establishment Bacon describes lies outside the powers of the state. Thus "the mystery of *New Atlantis,*" as Robert Faulkner comments, "culminates in the mystery of who governs."[24]

An examination of the text shows that Bacon frequently uses the term *state.* A recent study which analyzes the issues of governance and authority in New Atlantis offers a detailed summary of Bacon's various uses of the term in the *New Atlantis* and the different meanings he attributes to it. According to the author, the word state "occurs twenty-two times in *New Atlantis* (if one includes the three occurrences of 'estate'), and four different but connected meanings can be distinguished. Eight uses connote an active government. . . . Six uses (including two of 'estate') connote an established condition of living and progressing. . . . Six uses imply a condition of reverence. . . . Finally, two uses refer to Bensalem as a comprehensive whole, not limited to government or condition of life."[25] The author concludes, first, that the state in *New Atlantis* refers to a government that operates efficiently behind the scenes, second, that it is part of a broader establishment or a new condition of life and prosperity that we may call a society or perhaps a civilization, and third, that it represents a comprehensive state of mind about government and political authority. Another critic, Denise Albanese, has also remarked that the *New Atlantis* never explains its civil arrangements or structure of power. According to Albanese, "the text uses the words 'state' and 'kingdom' interchangeably, although the two words summon up images of government that pull (and would come to pull the more) in divergent directions: one is corporate, if faceless, the other incorporated by a titled head, known to all. . . . Bacon's advocacy of a revisionary philosophy of nature shifts the focus of his utopian text from the formalized study of human society to the systematized knowledge of an alien natural world."[26]

In sum, the *New Atlantis* offers no theory about the ordering of institutional structures in the state, nor about the origins and purpose of the state. The main emphasis in Bacon's ideal commonwealth is not on political arrangements but on a method for the investigation of nature. It is commonly agreed that in almost all of his writings Bacon gives a great deal of attention to his views on political philosophy. Yet nowhere does he develop a theory of the state or talk about a possible relationship between the state and nature in general or human nature in particular. The clue to why Bacon does not discuss such matters lies in his attitude toward nature. Rejecting the traditional doctrine of nature as fixed and immutable, and as controlling humankind, Bacon proposes a radically different way of perceiving nature and of viewing the connection between nature and human nature. Whereas in the Greek view nature was a model to be imitated, and in the Augustinian view it was something to be conquered by divine grace, in Bacon nature can be modified and transmuted, and it can be controlled by human beings.

From Bacon's perspective, nature does not reveal itself merely through observation or contemplation; on the contrary, it reveals its secrets only when subjected to a "variety of experiments."[27] For Plato and Aristotle, Augustine and More, nature is what it is; for Bacon we can act upon nature and thereby learn to control and fundamentally alter it. Thus the significant departure in Bacon is his view that by interfering with nature we learn how it works, how to dominate it, and how to improve it.[28] He insists that the older view of the universe as orderly and rational and, therefore, as totally comprehensible through reason alone, grew from the tendency to admire and extol the powers of the human mind. But, Bacon says, "the subtlety of nature is greater many times over than the subtlety of the senses and understanding, so that all those specious meditations, speculations, and glosses in which we indulge are quite from the purpose."[29] Accordingly, he proposes a new approach which provides the senses and understanding with the aids they need in order to properly interpret nature. Nature and the human mind act and react upon each other. And it is through this interaction between mind and nature that we gain knowledge about the physical world and, hence, mastery over it: "Human knowledge and human power meet in one, for where the cause is not known the effect cannot be produced. Nature to be commanded must be obeyed, and that which in contemplation is as the cause is in operation as the rule."[30] Given this approach to an explanation of the relation between human beings and the natural order, it is not surprising that Bacon would argue that "by the help and ministry of [humankind] a new face of bodies, another universe, . . . comes into view."[31] Bacon substitutes a new conception of the natural world and of our place in it for the Greek and Augustinian integrated and organically whole one. He rejects the idea that there is a correspondence between humanity and the cosmos and replaces it with a theory of nature that focuses not on the cosmos as a whole but on physical things as they are in themselves. For Bacon nature cannot be explained according to the notion that an intelligible rational order permeates the universe; rather it can only be explained according to principles we discover through the interaction between mind and nature. In a word, according to Bacon there are only the general principles of matter. Cosmic law, divine law, nature's law—all are replaced by Bacon with those principles of nature discovered by inquiry into the operations of discrete natural phenomena.

Nowhere is his departure from earlier ideas about nature more evident that in Bacon's rejection of the existing doctrine of "final causes." In Baconian thought the notion of final causes takes on an entirely new meaning. As we have seen, for Aristotle the final cause is in nature; for Augustine it is divine providence; for Bacon, on the other hand, the final cause has "relation clearly to [human] . . . nature rather than to the nature of the universe."[32] The final cause, then, is not in the natural world or in a supreme being:

> [Human beings], if we look to final causes, may be regarded as the center of the world; insomuch that if [they] were taken away from the world, the rest would seem to be all astray, without aim or purpose, . . . and leading to nothing. For the whole world works together in the service of humanity; and there is nothing from which we do not derive use and fruit . . . insomuch that all things seem to be going about humanity's business and not their own.[33]

Thus the important point here is the view that there are no final causes in nature, neither in nature in general nor in human nature. Nature serves the ends of humanity, not humanity the ends of nature. Human beings are the only final cause and the end is the thing they make; and, at the same time, the end for which things exist is created by human beings. From this perspective, final cause is determined not by teleological consequences, but by the results of our actions on nature. The main problem with the Aristotelian and Augustinian doctrines of final causes, according to Bacon, is that they start from an explanation of phenomena in terms of first principles outside the phenomena themselves. Aristotle and Augustine looked for final causes in the wrong place; final causes are not related to the universe but only to humanity. As Howard White has noted, "that which originally referred to the heavens or the cosmos refers, in Bacon, to humankind."[34]

This explains why Bacon never speaks of the origin or function of the state in the *New Atlantis*. For him the state is not, as with Aristotle, according to nature, or the consequence of our fallen nature, as with Augustine, or the result of natural human impulses, as with More. Rather, it is a human-made thing, an artificial product shaped and molded by human beings for no other purpose than the relief of their estate. Bacon comes nearer to More's outlook in his view of the state as a utilitarian instrument. But, unlike More, Bacon does not see human beings as having any instinctive leaning toward the state, or any natural tendency to create a rational political order which assumes a correspondence between humankind and the state. The departure in Bacon lay in his starting with the application of the experiential and inductive method to all areas of human affairs to the "effecting of all things possible." As he puts it in the *Magna Instauratio:* "There is but one course left therefore,—to try the whole thing anew upon a better plan, and to commence a total reconstruction of sciences, arts, and all human knowledge, raised upon the proper foundations."[35] On the basis of his own theory of knowledge, Bacon could not develop a concept of the state, and a political scheme for the conduct of human affairs could not be constructed, until social arrangements themselves had been systematically investigated according to his method. From this point of view, the *New Atlantis* is only a means to an end; the end itself is not yet known. The absence of a unifying social and political structure in *New Atlantis* corresponds to the incompleteness of the text itself—on the last page we are told that "the rest was not perfected." This change in point of view that we find in Bacon's utopian world regarding a comprehensive plan for social organization is in large measure the result of a break between one way of thinking about order and another.

A not surprising outcome of the Baconian philosophy of nature is a strikingly different approach to the concept of order. Given his overall perspective, it was inevitable that Bacon would reject the notion of the cosmos as an organically ordered whole intelligible to the human intellect. Since for Bacon nature is neither fixed nor immutable but something that can be controlled and fundamentally altered, order itself can be imposed by human beings. Bacon emphatically spurns the traditional view of nature as a coherent ordered whole that is under the control of a realm of Ideas and Forms or of divine providence. On this point, Stephen Collins, in his study of Baconian philosophy, notes that Bacon's ideas about order are, finally, time bound. As he says:

Bacon appreciated the union of aspiration and order. Methodologically, he suggested a means to direct our potential responsibility for order toward temporal ends. . . . His understanding of knowledge anchored the conceptualization of order to a methodology based upon an empirical appreciation of social reality. . . . Bacon's ordered universe contained eternal matter which was ever in flux. . . . His understanding of nature and of humankind helped define a new idea of order which no longer described a divine cosmos.[36]

Bacon rejects the Platonic and Aristotelian argument that an a priori order obtains throughout the universe and that it can be discerned by the human mind. In fact, for Bacon "the human understanding is of its own nature prone to suppose the existence of more order and regularity in the world than it finds."[37] For Bacon, nature does have some kind of order of its own, that is, is governed by some physical principles. And the order that nature does have is discovered by the human mind through careful observation and investigation of the particulars of natural phenomena: "All depends on keeping the eye steadily fixed upon the facts of nature and so receiving their images simply as they are. For God forbid that we should give out a dream of our own imagination for a pattern of the world."[38] Through the process of knowing we determine what kinds of order things have. Order is the product of the principles governing natural phenomena, and of our knowledge of, and therefore mastery over, nature.

The object of the whole of Bacon's thought was to establish the sovereignty of human beings over nature to the effecting of all things possible. And this sovereignty, Bacon argues, depends upon human knowledge. Yet, because there is a tendency in the human mind to error, that is, a predisposition of reason to superficiality which presents an obstacle to knowledge, we need a system of order, an ordered methodology that will direct us in our search for the truths of nature. "The understanding," Bacon says, "unless directed and assisted, is a thing unequal and quite unfit to contend with the obscurity of things."[39] Thus the sovereignty over nature is dependent upon human knowledge, and human knowledge is dependent upon an ordered process that will enable us to arrive at truth.

> But not only is a greater abundance of experiments to be
> sought for and procured, and that too of a different kind from
> those hitherto tried; an entirely different method, order, and
> process for carrying on and advancing experience must also
> be introduced. For experience, when it wanders in its own
> track, is, as I have already remarked, mere groping in the
> dark, and confounds rather than instructs us. But when it
> shall proceed in accordance with a fixed law, in regular order,
> and without interruption, then may better things be hoped of
> knowledge.[40]

Bacon's notion of order clearly centers on the idea that experience
must be directed and assisted "in accordance with a fixed law, in reg-
ular order, and without interruption" before "better things [can] be
hoped of knowledge." Accordingly, order for Bacon refers to a systematic arrangement of knowledge, and an organized method for the
investigation of nature. The need for and the purpose of an ordered
approach to knowledge is summarized by Bacon as follows:

> First of all we must prepare a natural and experimental his-
> tory, sufficient and good; and this is the foundation of all; for
> we are not to imagine or suppose, but to discover, what nature
> does or may be made to do. But natural and experimental his-
> tory is so various and diffuse, that it confounds and distracts
> the understanding, unless it be ranged and presented to view
> in a suitable order. We must therefore form tables and
> arrangements of instances, in such a method and order that
> the understanding may be able to deal with them. And even
> when this is done, still the understanding, if left to itself and
> its own spontaneous movements, is incompetent and unfit to
> form axioms, unless it be directed and guarded. Therefore in
> the third place we must use induction, true and legitimate in-
> duction, which is the very key of interpretation.[41]

But the real significance of Bacon's system does not lie in the fact
that he devised a new way of acquiring and organizing knowledge.
More important than this is Bacon's realization that the systematiza-

tion of data has significance only in terms of the possible abstractions that may be derived from the interpretation of specific classes of entities. As W. Donald Oliver points out in *Theory of Order*, while classification itself is an essential first step in the formation of abstract constructs, if it is to advance knowledge "it must not be practiced as an end in itself."[42] Oliver observes that the "great error" of scholastic philosophy "was the assumption that the process of abstraction comes to an end with the definition of a class."[43] And it is Bacon's recognition of this "error" that accounts for his achievement. His system of classification and his inductive method of reasoning make it possible to move from an observation of empirical data to generalizations that are probable rather than absolute; and, by a method of systematic investigation based on "proper rejections and exclusions,"[44] to the discovery of new generalizations. In short, the whole point of Bacon's system of organizing knowledge was that it was not an end in itself; on the contrary, it was to serve as the foundation upon which to "establish progressive stages of certainty."[45]

In summary, from the point of view of order the significant departure in Bacon's thought is the association of the idea of order with the acquisition of knowledge. In direct contrast to earlier notions of order that attempted to harmonize the whole of humankind and the cosmos, Bacon's theory of order attempts rather to harmonize humankind and the whole of human knowledge. An orderly method for acquiring knowledge leads to the discovery of the order in the phenomenal world. For Bacon, as one critic has put it, "nature created a conceptual order. Bacon's order was not definitive, rather it participated in the natural flux of things."[46] And, the continuous growth of knowledge leads to successive redefinitions of order. Since the order in nature is not given by an external will but consists in physical principles that are discovered by the human intellect, the order of natural entities is continuously reinterpreted as our knowledge of the phenomenal world advances.

For these reasons, Bacon does not propose in his *New Atlantis* the creation of a rationally ordered world that corresponds to a universal order that is stable, fixed, and organic. Order now is located in the principles of matter and it is to be discovered, and continuously redefined, through a careful observation and study of things as they are in themselves. Whereas More's *Utopia* offers a model upon which to build a rationally ordered social and political system, the *New Atlantis* offers a means to facilitate our search for ever-increasing knowledge of the secrets of the natural world. The *New Atlantis* thus embodies the visionary ideal of knowledge as progressive and of order as ever-changing. Finally, what Bacon gave to the concept of order was nothing less than its liberation from stagnation and from the uncompromising tension that resulted from the link between cosmic and temporal order.

Conclusion

In the preceding chapters we have seen that the idea of order is central to the meaning and purpose of classical utopianism. The distinguishing characteristic of traditional utopias is that they offer an insight into order, a clearly different vision of order that presents a challenge to the established way of explaining our involvement with the world. As our analysis has shown, Plato's vision of order in the *Republic* is challenged by Augustine in *The City of God*, and Augustine's vision of order is, in turn, challenged by More in the *Utopia*. And so too is More's vision of order challenged by Bacon in the *New Atlantis*.

It has also been pointed out that in spite of their differences the theories of order developed by Plato, Augustine, and More share two fundamental characteristics. First, they all view order as whole, fixed, and organic; and second, they hold that order is inseparable from purpose or ends. Thus while each may attribute the source of order to a different origin—for Plato it is intellect (Nous), for Augustine it is divine grace, and for More it is human nature—all three are at one in their view that order is immutable and teleological. Order, in other words, depends for its origin, its purpose, and its fulfillment upon a universal ordering principle. From this point of view, the supernatural order and the natural order, nature and human nature, mind and soul, are seen as one harmonious whole; order is a synthesis that integrates all phenomena, a unity that constitutes a perfect and total whole.

Thus from the Greek period until the seventeenth century, it is within the context of this general conception of universal order that all order was defined. In Plato's view, as we have noted, cosmic order provides the informing vision which guides us in our attempt to create the perfect political order. Although he arrives at dramatically different conclusions, Augustine too sees political order as bound up with cosmological order; the state is assigned its place and its purpose within a comprehensive and tightly structured system of divine universal order. Thomas More clearly stands apart from Plato and Augustine in that he does not propose a concept of order that establishes a determinate link between supernatural order and political order. Yet More still views order as organic and purposeful. More disengaged political order from cosmic order, but he did not abandon the notion that the order that exists in the temporal realm reflects an order that exists in the universe. And just as the total order of the universe is organic and teleological, so too is political order both a systematic whole and purposeful. Thus while More's view of order does not attempt to harmonize the total universe, it, nevertheless, remains a perfect and total system of political order within which the activities of human beings are blended into an harmonious whole on the one hand, and directed toward a clearly defined and specific *telos* on the other. As do Plato and Augustine, More, too, regards order as comprehensive, tightly structured, stable, and purposeful.

Thus More, in many respects, looks back to traditional ways of perceiving order; at the same time, he pointed the way toward the possibility of thinking about order as changeable rather than immutable, progressive rather than fixed. And this is precisely the point of view we find in the thought of Francis Bacon, who argues that order is progressive and that it consists of different kinds of order. As we saw in chapter 5, two elements in Bacon's ideas about nature point up the crucial differences between his views on order and those of his predecessors. The first is the notion that the universe is composed of disparate parts; it is not an organically ordered whole. The second is the idea that order has its origins in the interaction between mind and the phenomenal world. As we have seen, for Bacon order does not originate in the cosmos or in reason; order is not given, nor is it teleological. Knowledge of the physical principles that govern the phenomenal world makes human beings, not an external will, the determining agent of the meaning and purpose of order; and, as our knowledge of nature increases, we continuously rediscover new kinds of order. Order in Bacon is not viewed as perfect, stable, and all-inclusive; rather, it is seen as malleable, dynamic, and open-ended. In Bacon the idea of a cosmological order within which all phenomena are synthesized is abandoned; his preoccupation is with the discovery of actual and diverse kinds of order, with the discovery of the "natural" order in nature, and with the "making" of artificial orders. In a word, for Bacon order has been emancipated from cosmology.

It has been claimed that the modernity of More's *Utopia* rests in its challenge of capitalism and in its modern approach to the analysis of social problems and their solutions.[1] On the other hand, for J. H. Hexter "it is not the details that make *Utopia* modern; it is the bent of the spirit, the attitude of mind which informs and gives structure to those details."[2] I would suggest that the modernity of More's utopian vision is revealed in its engagement in political discourse and in More's role in Utopia as a political theorist who participates in the continuing historical dialogue on alternative and preferred possibilities for social order. In his study of the history of political theory, John Gunnell points out that a critical concern of political discourse, or, as he puts it, what continues to "haunt political theory," is the problem of actualization; that is, "the problem of how to transform social behavior and institutions in the image of a new vision of order."[3] Because More's ideas are presented within the context of utopian fiction it is a common mistake to misread his function in the *Utopia* as a political theorist and, in turn, his place in the history of political thought. Gunnell describes the role of the political theorist as follows: "Enjoined from political action in the ordinary sense, the theorist is satisfied with nothing less than political action in the extraordinary sense, that is, the role of author of a new order shaped in the author's own image."[4] There is little doubt that More saw himself in the *Utopia,* albeit somewhat reluctantly, as a political theorist, and as an architect of a new order, who is well aware of the gap between the words of his vision and their realization in the actual world.

Almost all scholars of utopianism acknowledge the modernity of Bacon's *New Atlantis,* and it is agreed that it rests in part on Bacon's adamant insistence that "the relief of our estate" depends upon the continual production of new knowledge. Charles Whitney, in *Francis Bacon and Modernity,* says that "this successful resistance to historical process through continuous discovery is thus really triumph over the necessity of having an historical consciousness, which must struggle with the fact that present conditions are different from past ones, and yet exist in a living relationship with them."[5] Despite all the conservatism in the *New Atlantis,* it is in this modern goal of narrowing and intensifying consciousness that we find a central aspect of Bacon's modernity as embodied in the scientific world he creates in Bensalem. Bensalemites achieve liberation from the compromising tension between tradition and innovation precisely because they produce new knowledge on the one hand, and because this knowledge empowers them on the other. In Bacon's words, "human knowledge and human power meet in one." It is the privileging of the advancement of knowledge that makes Bacon's utopian discourse unique and which gives the *New Atlantis* one of its most distinctively modern characteristics.

More directly relevant to our purpose is an interpretation of the new attitude toward order in the seventeenth century that is given by Stephen Collins in his study *From Divine Cosmos to Sovereign State.* Collins says: "A change in the idea of order is a change in consciousness. The self-defined, articulated, representative order contextualized in the mid-seventeenth century signified the development of self-consciousness. Order now resided in definition, in the conscious naming of things which reduced objective reality to a series of identities. Order was no longer a perception of consciousness; it was now a responsible articulation of the self-consciousness of consciousness."[6] This emphasis, Collins adds, and as we have already seen, "led to an abandonment of that mode of discourse founded on the paradigm of resemblance which defined the traditional idea of order."[7] As we discussed in detail in chapter 5, what Collins describes is exactly the attitude toward order that Bacon expresses in his utopia and the way he defines it in his other writings. It will be recalled that in the *Magna Instauratio* he tells us: "All depends on keeping the eye steadily fixed upon the facts of nature and so receiving their images simply as they are. For God forbid that we should give out a dream of our own imagination for a pattern of the world."[8] Order in Bacon is located in disparate particulars and in definition and it is to be discovered, and continuously redefined, through a careful observation and study of things as they are in themselves. In direct contrast to More and earlier utopian writers we have examined in this book, order for Bacon is, in a word, spatial, not closed. Within this context it is clear that the modernity of the *New Atlantis* is not solely, as some have suggested, in its insistence on the transformative power of scientific investigation, nor in its proposal for an egalitarian realignment of social systems in order to achieve greater social harmony. In point of fact, its modernity is first and foremost in its idea that order is open-ended and, concomitantly, that it is always in the process of redefining itself.

It has been my purpose in this study to examine the relation between classical utopianism and the history of the idea of order.[9] I have argued in the course of this book that classical utopianism shares a defining affinity with the notion of order, and I have shown that this affinity has been generally ignored in the dialogue on utopianism. My argument has also linked the demise of classical utopianism with the radically new definition of order that took hold in the seventeenth century. As I have pointed out, some scholars, in commenting on the decline in classical utopianism, argue that it resulted from the fact that the social and political institutions being proposed were impractical, or, that the proposed ideas about human experiences presented in various utopian visions were incompatible with the true nature and needs of humankind. And others, as I mentioned in the introduction, claim that it resulted from the new emphasis on scientific inquiry in all areas of human thought. While such explanations have their place in the overall study of utopianism, they fail to persuade completely. This study argues that the principal reason for the disappearance of classical utopianism lies in the fundamental change in attitude toward order; the shift in outlook concerning the idea of order, in other words, coincides with the demise of classical utopianism. As we have seen, the new approach to the idea of order served, among other things, to dissolve completely the classical and medieval synthesis. We can only conclude, I think, that in giving up the idea of order as immutable and teleological, and the accompanying belief that the ideal political order mirrors the order of the cosmos, Bacon and his contemporaries, especially Bacon by means of the open-ended utopian vision that he presents in his *New Atlantis,* deprived classical utopianism of its central informing vision.

Notes

Introduction

1. See, for example, Glenn Negley and J. Max Patrick, eds., *The Quest for Utopia: An Anthology of Imaginary Societies* (New York: Henry Schuman, 1952). Negley and Patrick draw a distinction between "ideal" and "practical" utopias, and among other examples they classify More's *Utopia* as an "ideal" utopia and works of the Italian Renaissance city-planners as "practical" utopias. Perhaps the fact that the traditional utopia is almost always presented within the framework of a well-designed city explains why critics include the works of the Italian Renaissance town-planners as utopian examples. But the city the utopist describes is actually the means through which the idea of an ideal is presented; in utopia the focus is consistently on guiding principles, not on the physical design of a city. For an excellent discussion of the "ideal city" in the Italian Renaissance see Eugenio Garin, *Science and Civic Life in the Italian Renaissance*, trans. Peter Munz (New York: Doubleday, 1969), 21-48.
2. Lewis Mumford, *The Story of Utopias* (New York: Viking Press, 1922), 15.
3. Joyce O. Hertzler, *The History of Utopian Thought* (New York: Macmillan, 1926), 2-3, 7.
4. S. B. Liljegren, *Studies on the Origin and Early Tradition of English Utopian Fiction* (Copenhagen: Uppsala University Press, 1961), 16.
5. Robert C. Elliott, *The Shape of Utopia: Studies in a Literary Genre* (Chicago: University of Chicago Press, 1970), 7.
6. Karl Mannheim, *Ideology and Utopia: An Introduction to the Sociology of Knowledge,* trans. Louis Wirth and Edward Shils (New York: Harcourt Brace, 1940), 173-81.
7. Paul Tillich, "Critique and Justification of Utopia," in *Utopias and Utopian Thought,* ed. Frank E. Manuel (Boston: Beacon Press, 1967), 298, 300-302.
8. Frank E. Manuel, "Toward a Psychological History of Utopias," in *Utopias and Utopian Thought,* 69, 71-72.
9. Northrup Frye, "Varieties of Literary Utopias," in *Utopias and Utopian Thought,* 25, 39, 42, 48. In Christianity, Frye suggests, "instead of utopia we have the City of God, a utopian metaphor most elaborately developed in St. Augustine. . . . The attainment of the City of God in literature must be classified as a form of utopian fiction, its most famous literary treatment being the *Purgatorio* and *Paradiso* of Dante," 34.

10. Ernest L. Tuveson, *Millennium and Utopia: A Study in the Background of the Idea of Progress* (New York: Harper & Row, 1964), ix-x.

11. Frank E. Manuel and Fritzie P. Manuel, *Utopian Thought in the Western World* (Cambridge: Harvard University Press, 1979), 5. In his extensive and wide-ranging study of utopianism, Ernst Bloch too proposes a broad definition of utopia. Bloch includes, for example, day-dreams, myths, fairy tales, literary utopias, the bible, Augustine's *The City of God,* and the voyages of sea-travelers. According to Bloch, there is a utopian impulse in human nature that he defines as "anticipatory consciousness," or, a creative source of material always on the verge of coming to consciousness (11, v.1). "The anticipatory thus operates in the field of hope; so this hope is not taken *only as emotion,* . . . but *more essentially as a directing act of a cognitive kind.* . . .The imagination and the thoughts of future intention described in this way are utopian" (12, v.1; emphasis in original). *The Principle of Hope.* 3 vols., trans. Neville Plaice, Stephen Plaice, and Paul Knight (Cambridge, MA: MIT Press, 1986; first published in 1967).

12. Krishan Kumar, *Utopianism* (Minneapolis: University of Minnesota Press, 1991), 17. At another point in his study Kumar argues that there is no tradition of utopia and utopian thought outside the Western world. "Other varieties of the ideal society or the perfect condition of humanity are to be found in abundance in non-Western societies, usually embedded in religious cosmologies. But nowhere in these societies do we find the practice of writing utopias, of criticizing them, of developing and transforming their themes and exploring new possibilities within them. Even if individual works can be found with some of the hallmarks of the Western utopia—and that too can be disputed—there is no utopian tradition of thought" (33). However, Lyman Tower Sargent argues that "utopias are not solely the product of the Christian West, but utopias as a genre of literature that has certain formal characteristics are most common in the West, almost certainly because the genre is identified with Thomas More, a person from the Christian West." "The Three Faces of Utopianism Revisited," *Utopian Studies* 5 (1994): 2.

13. Kumar, *Utopianism,* 87-88.

14. Timothy Kenyon, *Utopian Communism and Political Thought in Early Modern England* (London: Pinter Publishers, 1989), vii, 17.

15. See, for example, Raymond Ruyer, *L'utopie et les utopies* (Paris: Presses Universitaires de France, 1950); Richard Gerber, *Utopian Fantasy* (London: Routledge & Paul, 1955); and Darko Suvin, "Defining the Literary Genre of Utopia," *Studies in the Literary Imagination* 6 (Fall 1973): 121-45.

16. Bertrand de Jouvenel, "Utopia for Practical Purposes," in *Utopias and Utopian Thought,* 221.

17. Excellent discussions of Platonic and Aristotelian thought on the notion of cosmic order and harmony are to be found in Ernan McMullin, "Cosmic Order in Plato and Aristotle," in *The Concept of Order*, ed. Paul G. Kuntz (Seattle, WA: University of Washington Press, 1968), 63-76; George H. Sabine, *A History of Political Theory*, 3rd ed. (New York: Holt, Rhinehart, and Winston, 1961); Leo Strauss and Joseph Cropsey, eds., *History of Political Philosophy*, 2nd ed. (Chicago: Rand McNally, 1972); Charles H. McIlwain, *The Growth of Political Thought in the West: From the Greeks to the End of the Middle Ages* (New York: Macmillan, 1932); Ernest Barker, *Greek Political Theory: Plato and His Predecessors* (New York: Barnes and Noble, 1918).

18. Arthur O. Lovejoy, *The Great Chain of Being: A Study of the History of an Idea* (New York: Harper and Row, 1936), 35.

19. It should be mentioned that the demiurge of Plato, like the First Mover of Aristotle and the One of Plotinus, transcends things only in a relative manner. As one finite being, albeit highest, among other finites, it does not and cannot exist apart from the universe. In contrast, the creator-God of Augustine is absolutely transcendent. He is, in the medieval phrase, "non de hoc mundo." As infinite, he is wholly other than and totally independent of the finites he creates. For a discussion of this topic the works cited in note 17 above should be consulted.

20. See McMullin, "Cosmic Order in Plato and Aristotle," 63-76.

21. For a discussion of the notion of order in Buddhism see Edward Conze, "Dharma as a Spiritual, Social, and Cosmic Force," in *The Concept of Order*, ed. Kuntz, 239-52.

22. Henri Frankfort, et al., *Before Philosophy: The Intellectual Adventure of Ancient Man* (Baltimore, MD: Penguin, 1949), 67. This excellent study of the thought of the ancient Near East should be consulted for an extensive treatment of the way in which the ancients regarded their world. The main thesis of the work is that in Egyptian and Mesopotamian cosmology the world appears "neither inanimate nor empty but redundant with life; and life has individuality, in [humankind] and beast and plant, and in every phenomenon. . . . Any phenomenon may at any time face us, not as 'it,' but as 'Thou.' In this confrontation, 'Thou' reveals its individuality, its qualities, its will. 'Thou' is not contemplated with intellectual detachment; it is experienced as life confronting life, involving every faculty in a reciprocal relationship. Thoughts, no less than acts and feelings, are subordinated to this experience," 14.

23. Frankfort, et al., *Before Philosophy*, 139.

24. See note 19 above.

25. Augustine, *De civitate Dei*, trans. George E. McCracken, et al. 7 vols. (Cambridge, MA: Harvard University Press, 1957-1972), bk. 19, ch. 13, vol. 6:175.

26. Thomas Aquinas, *Summa contra gentiles,* in *The Basic Writings of Saint Thomas Aquinas,* trans. and ed. Anton C. Pegis, 2 vols. (New York: Random House, 1945), bk. 3, ch. 81, vol. 2:153.

27. *Summa contra gentiles,* bk. 3, ch. 69, vol. 2:126.

28. The metaphor of order as a "vast chain of being" served to express, as E. M. W. Tillyard puts it, "the unimaginable plenitude of God's creation, its unfaltering order, and its ultimate unity. The chain stretched from the foot of God's throne to the meanest of inanimate objects. Every speck of creation was a link in the chain, and every link except those at the two extremities was simultaneously bigger and smaller than another: there could be no gap." *The Elizabethan World Picture: A Study of the Idea of Order in the Age of Shakespeare, Donne, and Milton* (New York: Random House, n.d.), 26.

29. Rudolf Arnheim, *Entropy and Art: An Essay on Disorder and Order* (Berkeley: University of California Press, 1971), 48.

30. Paul G. Kuntz, "The Necessity and Universality of Hierarchical Thought," in Paul G. Kuntz and Marion Leathers Kuntz, eds., *Jacob's Ladder and the Tree of Life: Concepts of Hierarchy and the Great Chain of Being* (New York: Peter Lang Publishing, 1987), 8. In his study of the concept of order, Eric Voegelin writes: "Every society is burdened with the task, under its concrete conditions, of creating an order that will endow the fact of its existence with meaning in terms of ends divine and human. . . .The truth of order has to be gained and regained in the perpetual struggle against the fall from it; and the movement toward truth starts from an awareness of one's existence in untruth." *Order and History,* 4 vols. (Baton Rouge: Louisiana State University Press, 1956-1974), vol. 1, ix, xiv. From this perspective, it can be seen that classical utopianism at one and the same time offered a new explanation of order and in the process revealed the "untruths" about the prevailing ordering vision.

31. Keith Booker, *The Dystopian Impulse in Modern Literature* (Westport, CT: Greenwood Press, 1994), 14.

32. Ruth Levitas, *The Concept of Utopia* (Hemel Hempstead, Eng.: Philip Allan, 1990), 4.

33. Levitas, 4.

34. Levitas, 5.

35. Levitas, 5.

36. Levitas, 8. Besides the work of Levitas see also Lucy Sargisson, *Contemporary Feminist Utopianism* (New York: Routledge, 1996) for a definition of utopia that incorporates yet goes considerably beyond the view expressed by Levitas. Sargisson's work is a study of contemporary feminist utopian thought in which she argues for a "new" approach to utopianism that fo-

cuses not on perfection and closure but, rather, on dynamism and unending process. As she summarizes it: "I have argued in the course of this book that utopianism needs to be reapproached, because the view of utopian thought as closed and enclosing is inappropriate to what has been identified as the new (and radical) transgressive utopianism emerging from feminism and other contemporary discourses, as well as being inappropriate to many historical utopias. My argument has linked approach and conceptualization, and through a *different* approach to utopian thought I have created and practiced what I call a new utopianism—the concept is (in)formed by the process of openended conceptualization. My approach is embedded in contemporary feminisms and is informed by the transgressive discourses of Derridean and Cixousian poststructuralism. My conclusion, if you like, is that the new utopianism represents the manifestation of a conscious and necessary desire to resist the closure that is evoked by approaches to utopia as perfect, and that has far-reaching implications. Transgressive utopianism is, for instance, of a political nature, but is fundamentally transgressive of not only the political present but also the ways in which it is normally studied. Feminist political theory, for instance, has broadened the meaning of the concept of politics—feminist content-based analyses illustrate this point quite adequately, and near-unanimity exists amongst commentators as to the political concerns of women" (226-27; emphasis in original). Sargisson's essential argument is that contemporary feminist political theory has broadened the meaning of the concept of politics precisely because it focuses on process, on the one hand, and resists closure on the other. This radical shift in perspective results in a dynamic, openended and transgressive utopian text that offers new understandings of and approaches to politics.

37. Judith Shklar, "The Political Theory of Utopia: From Melancholy to Nostalgia," in *Utopias and Utopian Thought*, 103.

Chapter 1
Paradise vs. Utopia: Augustine's *The City of God*

Sections of this chapter appeared in "Reconsidering the Ideal: *The City of God* and Utopian Speculation," in *The City of God: A Collection of Critical Essays*, ed. Dorothy F. Donnelly (New York: Peter Lang Publishing, 1995): 199-211.

1. Augustine, *The Retractations*, trans. Mary I. Bogan, R. S. M. (Washington: Catholic University Press, 1968), 209-10.

2. Augustine, *De civitate Dei,* trans. George E. McCracken, et al. 7 vols. (Cambridge, MA: Harvard University Press, 1957-1972), bk. 11, ch. 1, vol. 3:427. The form in which Augustine expresses the dualism of existence, that is, the conceptualization of "two cities," antedates the composition of *The City of God.* The idea is found in Stoicism, for example, in Marcus Aurelius's *Meditations,* and in Cicero and Seneca. It is also found in the Old and New Testaments. But its most explicit development is in the *Commentary on the Apocalypse* written by Tyconius, a Donatist priest. Tyconius's use of the idea is most often spoken of as Augustine's source of the overall frame for his work. See trans. note, *The Retractations,* 213.

3. *De civ. Dei,* bk. 14, ch. 1, vol. 4:259-61.

4. *De civ. Dei,* bk. 15, ch. 1, vol. 4:411-13.

5. *De civ. Dei,* bk. 14, ch. 28, vol. 4:405.

6. In *The City of God* Augustine presents a lengthy discussion of contemporary philosophical thought in which he challenges the ideas of Varro, Pythagoras, and Porphyry, among others, but, he points out that "theology must be discussed above all with the Platonists, for their opinion is preferable to the creeds of all other philosophers" (bk. 8, ch. 5, vol. 3:23). And from Augustine's point of view the philosopher who was most acceptable was Plato, for it is he who "was able to acquire the understanding by which he came near to Christian knowledge" (bk. 8, ch. 11, vol. 3:51).

7. For excellent discussions of the historical development of the theme of "otherworldliness" and "this-worldliness" see Arthur O. Lovejoy, *The Great Chain of Being: A Study of the History of an Idea* (New York: Harper & Row, 1936), and Paul G. Kuntz and Marion Leathers Kuntz, eds., *Jacob's Ladder and the Tree of Life: Concepts of Hierarchy and the Great Chain of Being* (New York: Peter Lang Publishing, 1987).

8. While it is generally recognized that as Plato's thought developed he became more interested in the theological implications of his Theory of Ideas, his views nonetheless remained sharply different from the Christian outlook. Plato, as Gordon Leff observes, "accorded no place to a creator; there was no explanation of the way the forms came into being or whither they led; there was no sense of movement or development, but simply a timeless process without *raison d'être;* there was no eschatology: the soul itself pre-existed and migrated to different bodies, but it never met a last judgment or an eternal life." *Medieval Thought: St. Augustine to Ockham* (Baltimore: Penguin, 1958), 13-14. See also Lovejoy, *The Great Chain of Being,* 41-48.

9. *De civ Dei,* bk. 12, ch. 2, vol. 4:11.

10. *De civ. Dei*, bk. 21, ch. 5, vol. 7:24; bk. 21, ch. 6, vol. 7:34.

11. Lovejoy, *The Great Chain of Being*, 38.

12. P. R. L. Brown, "St. Augustine," in *Trends in Medieval Political Thought*, ed. Beryl Smalley (Oxford: Basil Blackwell, 1965), 2.

13. See *De civ. Dei*, bk. 11, ch. 10, vol. 3:463-71; bk. 12, ch. 2, vol. 4:9-13.

14. *De civ. Dei*, bk. 12, ch. 21, vol. 4:105.

15. For a comprehensive and insightful discussion of Platonic thought consult Francis MacDonald Cornford, *Plato's Theory of Knowledge* (New York: Humanities Press, 1951).

16. Not unexpectedly, this shift in perspective on the concept of order resulted in a new explanation of the meaning of "membership" that was to have a profound impact on the notion of political association and, in turn, on the theory of political obligation. For a full discussion of this idea see Sheldon S. Wolin, *Politics and Vision: Continuity and Innovation in Western Political Thought* (Boston: Little Brown, 1960). Wolin offers an excellent discussion of the revolutionary challenge to the idea of "membership" posed by the disintegration of the Greek *polis*. Wolin traces the change in the meaning of membership from the Hellenistic period down to the Roman writers of the early Christian era. I am indebted to Wolin's chapters on "Space and Community" and "Time and Community."

17. It has been suggested that in Platonic thought we can "treat the good as simply being rational order, and all the other forms as simply being particular types of rational order. . . . If the good simply is rational order, it is at least intelligible that this should be so. A form is the ontological correlate of the correct answer to the question *ti esti?* or 'what is it?' asked about a property or universal. . . . The form of justice is an instance of rational order, then, but it is also a part of a larger structure which itself exhibits rational order." See C. D. C. Reeve, "Platonic Politics and the Good," *Political Theory* 23 (1995): 417-18.

18. *De civ. Dei*, bk. 22, ch. 30, vol. 7:373.

19. For an extended discussion of this point the following works should be consulted. Robert A. Markus, "Two Conceptions of Political Authority: Augustine, *De Civitate Dei*, XIX. 14-15, and Some Thirteenth-Century Interpretations," *Journal of Theological Studies* 16 (1965): 68-100; Oliver O'Donovan, "Augustine's *City of God* XIX and Western Political Thought," *Dionysius* 11 (1987): 89-110; Peter Brown, *Augustine of Hippo: A Biography* (London: Faber & Faber, 1967); Herbert A. Deane, *The Political and Social Ideas of St. Augustine* (New York: Columbia University Press, 1963).

20. *De civ. Dei*, bk. 15, ch. 1, vol. 4:411-13.

21. *De civ. Dei*, bk. 12, ch. 1, vol. 4:3.

22. *De civ. Dei,* bk. 19, ch. 21, vol. 6:207. On the idea of the relationship between justice and a collective community of interest, Christopher Bruell says that for Plato justice takes as its starting point the idea that "justice demands of us devotion to the common good, together with the opinion that the common good is, for most practical purposes, identical with the good of the city, or the political community. . . . If justice consists . . . in service to the political community, the question of the goodness of justice can almost be reduced to the question of the goodness of such service" (272-73). "On Plato's Political Philosophy," *The Review of Politics* (Spring 1994): 261-82.

23. *De civ. Dei,* bk. 19, ch. 21, vol. 6:207-209.

24. *De civ. Dei,* bk. 19, ch. 21, vol. 6:209.

25. *De civ. Dei,* bk. 19, ch. 21, vol. 6:209.

26. *De civ. Dei,* bk. 19, ch. 21, vol. 6:209.

27. *De civ. Dei,* bk. 19, ch. 21, vol. 6:211.

28. *De civ. Dei,* bk. 2, ch. 21, vol. 1:225-27.

29. *De civ. Dei,* bk. 19, ch. 23, vol. 6:231.

30. Quoted in C. Dawson, "Saint Augustine and His Age," *A Monument to Saint Augustine: Essays on Some Aspects of His Thought,* ed. M. C. D'Arcy, et al. (London: Sheed & Ward, 1930), 53.

31. *De civ. Dei,* bk. 11, ch. 1, vol. 3:427. For the argument that Augustine locates the origins of political authority in the fall, and the view that the justification for political authority is embedded in the doctrine of predestination, see Dino Bigongiari, "The Political Ideas of St. Augustine," in *Essays on Dante and Medieval Culture: Critical Studies of the Thought and Texts of Dante, St. Augustine, Marsilius of Padua, and Other Medieval Subjects* (Firenze: L. S. Olschki, 1964); Norman H. Baynes, *The Political Ideas of St. Augustine's* De Civitate Dei (London: The Historical Association, 1936); John N. Figgis, *The Political Aspects of St. Augustine's* City of God (London: Longmans & Green, 1921). For the claim that "book x, chapter 13, of *The City of God* is an eloquent piece of evidence that Augustine attributed at least a limited degree of genuine moral probity to historical societies not favored by divine revelation," see Jeremy D. Adams, "Augustine's Definitions of *Populus* and the Value of Society," in *The Populus of Augustine and Jerome: A Study in the Patristic Sense of Community* (New Haven, CT: Yale University Press, 1971), 134.

32. *De civ. Dei,* bk. 5, ch. 11, vol. 2:189.

33. *De civ. Dei,* bk. 5, ch. 21, vol. 2: 249-51.

34. *De civ. Dei,* bk. 19, ch. 24, vol. 6:233.

35. See book 19 of *De civ. Dei* for a full discussion of this point.

36. *De civ. Dei*, bk. 19, ch. 26, vol. 6:237.
37. Elaine Pagels, "The Politics of Paradise," *Harvard Theological Review* 78 (1985): 67, 80. In contrast to the general scholarly consensus on Augustine's doctrine of obedience, including the generally accepted argument as presented, for example, by P. R. L. Brown, that in Augustine it requires strict obedience to even unjust civil authority (5), Peter Burnell proposes that "in principle Augustine's view of civil life is not . . . static. It does not make endless cooperation with wickedness a necessary concomitant of a Christian's civil duties. Though a long way from the sort of 'liberation theology' that regards the Gospel as predominantly political, Augustine's position implicitly allows for considerable development in radically reformative or even revolutionary political directions. Such development would of course be quite foreign to his 'politics' but not to his principles." "The Problem of Service to Unjust Regimes in Augustine's *City of God*," *Journal of the History of Ideas* 54 (1993): 187.
38. *De civ. Dei*, bk. 14, ch. 12, vol. 4:335.
39. *De civ. Dei*, bk. 19, ch. 14, vol. 6:181.
40. Wolin, *Politics and Vision*, 125.
41. *De civ. Dei*, bk. 5, ch. 17, vol. 2:219.
42. In his study of Western political thought Wolin observes that "in the Augustinian conception of time one of the most original and significant contributions of Christian thought was given its classic statement. There were enormous political implications in the new notion of time, implications which did much to delineate the contrasts between the classical and Christian attitudes towards political problems" (123). See also Karl Löwith, *Meaning in History: The Theological Implications of the Philosophy of History* (Chicago: University of Chicago Press, 1949). Löwith says that Augustine's "final argument against the classical concept of time is . . . a moral one: the pagan doctrine is hopeless, for hope and faith are essentially related to the future and a real future cannot exist if past and future times are equal phases within a cyclic recurrence without beginning and end" (163).

Chapter 2
Sacred and Secular Order: Aquinas and the Body Politic

An earlier version of this chapter appeared as "Aquinas and Some Subsequent Thinkers on the Renewal of Utopian Speculation," in *The Thomist* 46 (1982): 539-72.

1. Paul J. Weithman, "Augustine and Aquinas on Original Sin and the Function of Political Authority," *Journal of the History of Philosophy* 30 (1992): 353-76. For an excellent discussion of the many substantial differences between Augustine and Aquinas concerning especially their political thought, see Weithman's insightful analysis of their opposing views on political authority and subjection, the value of the common good, the purpose of earthly peace, and the notion of obedience.

2. Thomas Aquinas, *Summa theologiae*, Blackfriars' ed. and trans. (New York: McGraw-Hill, 1964), 1, q. 108, art. 2, vol. 14:127.

3. *Summa theologiae*, 1, q. 108, art. 1, vol. 14:123.

4. *Summa theologiae*, 1-2, q. 109, art. 1, vol. 30:71.

5. Walter Ullmann, *A History of Political Thought: The Middle Ages* (Baltimore, MD: Penguin, 1965), 182. For a full discussion of the influence of Aristotelian thought on the political ideas of Aquinas see esp. 167-73; ch. 7.

6. *Aristotle's Politics*, trans. Benjamin Lowett, introd. H. W. C. Davis (London: Oxford University Press, 1931), 40, 28, 40.

7. *Aristotle's Politics*, 34, 292.

8. *Aristotle's Politics*, 119-20, 290-91.

9. *Aristotle's Politics*, 106.

10. *Summa theologiae*, 1-2, q. 72, art. 4, vol. 25:39.

11. Dino Bigongiari, "The Political Ideas of St. Thomas Aquinas," in *Essays on Dante and Medieval Culture: Critical Studies of the Thought and Texts of Dante, St. Augustine, St. Thomas Aquinas, Marsilius of Padua, and Other Medieval Subjects* (Firenze: L. S. Olschki, 1964), 106.

12. Thomas Aquinas, *On Princely Government*, in *Aquinas: Selected Political Writings*, trans. and ed. A. P. D'Entréves (Oxford: Basil Blackwell, 1948), 3-5.

13. Thomas Aquinas, *Commentary on the Politics of Aristotle*, in *Aquinas: Selected Political Writings*, 197.

14. *Summa theologiae*, 2-2, q. 10, art. 10, vol. 32:69.

15. Thomas Aquinas, *Commentary on the Sentences of Peter Lombard*, in *Aquinas: Selected Political Writings*, 187. In Aquinas's thought the church has an indirect power in temporal matters, but it exercises its authority in temporal affairs only in so far as they relate to the supernatural. In his introduction D'Entréves presents an insightful study of Aquinas's political thought that should be consulted for a discussion of Aquinas's views on the relationship between the church and the state.

16. Thomas Aquinas, *Commentary on the Nicomachean Ethics*, in *Aquinas: Selected Political Writings*, 191. For a thoughtful analysis of Aquinas's use

of the term *society* see I. Th. Eschmann, "Studies on the Notion of Society in St. Thomas Aquinas," *Mediaeval Studies* 8 (1946): 1-42.

17. Gordon Leff, *Medieval Thought: St. Augustine to Ockham* (Baltimore: Penguin, 1958), 251.

18. Henry Bamford Parkes, *The Divine Order* (New York: Alfred A. Knopf, 1969), 259-60.

19. Ullmann, *A History of Political Thought,* 176.

20. Aquinas, *Commentary on the Politics of Aristotle,* 195-97.

21. Wolin, *Politics and Vision,* 139.

22. A. P. D'Entréves, ed. *Aquinas: Selected Political Writings,* xv.

23. In his analysis of late Medieval thought, Parkes points out that the most important "new threat to Christian doctrine was the growing influence of Aristotle, who reached the West through Arabic intermediaries and accompanied by Arabic interpretations, especially those of the twelfth-century Spanish philosopher Ibn Rochd, generally known to the West as Averroes . . . . The West was now being introduced to a system of thought which affirmed that philosophy was independent of theology and might arrive at truths contrary to those of religion. According to Averroes there were two kinds of truth, each of them valid in its own sphere. . . . During the second half of the thirteenth century, . . . scholastic philosophers began to incorporate Aristotelian doctrines into Christianity, making a distinction between truths accessible to the human reason and truths that could be known only through revelation. The two forms of truth were not in contradiction with each other, but were known through different channels," 250-52.

24. In his discussion of the concept of natural law in Aquinas's thought, Edgar Scully argues that "although natural law is fundamental to the whole of St. Thomas's political philosophy, positive civil law, as the vehicle through which the state is governed, is, for him, something super-added and imposed from without by human authority. As such, it is distinct from natural law, which stems from the inner animality of [the person]. It comes into being through experience, prudence, and art, not by way of inference from natural law. Insofar as its end is the common good of the community as a whole, it bears merely upon the external acts of virtue in all its forms required by natural law. Its essential meaning as 'positive' law, that is, as law 'posited' or 'laid down,' in this instance, by *human* authority, is best seen from the viewpoint of those civil laws that are morally neutral and purely regulative in character, not from the viewpoint of those civil laws having a moral content coinciding with natural law." "The Political Limitations of Natural Law in Aquinas," in *The Medieval Tradition of Natural Law,* ed.

Harold J. Johnson (Kalamazoo, MI: Western Michigan University Press, 1987), 154.

25. Parkes, *The Divine Order,* 250. Gordon Leff puts it this way: "The fourteenth century carries no direct impress of the thirteenth. It is not, like the latter, an age of syntheses. . . . It is preoccupied with the limits, rather than the scope of reason; its thinkers devoted themselves to definition rather than to construction," 261.

26. Ullmann, *A History of Political Thought,* 184-85.

27. See note 23 above.

Chapter 3
Redeeming Utopia: Dante's *De Monarchia*
and Marsilius's *Defensor Pacis*

1. The separation of the secular from the spiritual, and of faith from reason, that we find in both Dante and Marsilius, and later in many fourteenth-century thinkers, is often ascribed to Averroism. Averroes (1126-1178) argued that faith and reason operate at different levels and that they do not inform each other. Although Aquinas was influenced by Averroes in his separation of faith and reason, Aquinas's purpose was to better harmonize philosophy and theology. Averroes, on the other hand, denied an ultimate harmony between faith and reason. In Dante and Marsilius also, as we see, the emphasis is on differentiation not synthesis, and on the notion that there exist two separate ends for human beings, and that these ends are achieved by different means. See Etienne Gilson, "Dante's Place in History," in *Critical Essays on Dante,* ed. Giuseppe Mazzotta (Boston: G. K. Hall, 1991), 119-38. Gilson offers an insightful discussion of the influence of Averroism on the ideas found in the *Monarchia.* As Gilson puts it, "it is . . . legitimate to wonder whether, by virtue of the principles from which it draws its inspiration and the use to which it puts them, Dante's *Monarchy* is not itself in some way, and even, perhaps, in a very original way, one of the expressions of mediaeval Latin Averroism" (128). See also Henry Bamford Parkes, *The Divine Order* (New York: Alfred A. Knopf, 1969), 150-51. And Donna Mancusi-Ungaro, in her extremely competent study, *Dante and the Empire* (New York: Peter Lang Publishing, 1987), provides a detailed and thoughtful treatment of the relationship between Averroism and the *Monarchy.* See especially 129-50.

2. Gordon Leff, *Medieval Thought: St. Augustine To Ockham* (Baltimore: Penguin, 1958), 258. For an extended discussion of the thought of Duns Scotus see 255-72.

3. It should be pointed out that the changing concept of the relationship between faith and reason was not, as it might seem, an attempt to refute theological doctrine. On the contrary, the tenets of Christianity were as fundamental for Dante, Marsilius, and Duns Scotus in the fourteenth century as they were for Augustine in the fifth and, indeed, as they were, for example, for most seventeenth-century thinkers. In his study of seventeenth-century thought Basil Willey points out that "it was one of the characteristics of the seventeenth century that no English writer of the time, whatever his philosophical views might be, could explicitly abandon the assumption that the universe rested upon a basis of divine meaning. Further, all thinkers of that century, with but one or two exceptions, assumed the truth in some sense of the specifically Christian doctrines, and the supernatural status of the Bible." *The Seventeenth-Century Background* (New York: Columbia University Press, 1965), 111. Although a quite different spirit animates the thought of the seventeenth century, it is out of the fourteenth-century background that most thinkers of the later period resolve the conflict between two incompatible worldviews by proposing that truth is twofold.

4. Dante Alighieri, *De Monarchia,* trans. Herbert W. Schneider, introd. Dino Bigongiari (New York: Liberal Arts Press, 1949), bk. 1, ch. 2, 4-5.

5. *De Monarchia,* bk. 1, ch. 3, 6; bk. 1, ch. 4, 7.

6. *De Monarchia,* bk. 1, ch. 4, 7.

7. *De Monarchia,* bk. 1, ch. 8, 11.

8. *De Monarchia,* bk. 2, ch. 1, 24.

9. *De Monarchia,* bk. 2, ch. 3, 27.

10. *De Monarchia,* bk. 2, ch. 5, 32.

11. *De Monarchia,* bk. 2, ch. 5, 33.

12. *De Monarchia,* bk. 2, ch. 6, 37.

13. *De Monarchia,* bk. 3, ch. 16, 80.

14. *De Monarchia,* bk. 3, ch. 16, 78.

15. *De Monarchia,* bk. 1, ch. 3, 5-6.

16. *De Monarchia,* bk. 1, ch. 3, 6.

17. *De Monarchia,* bk. 3, ch. 4, 59-60.

18. *De Monarchia,* bk. 1, ch. 6, 9-10.

19. In discussing the similarities and differences between Dante's *Commedia* and *Monarchia,* Ascoli argues that "the basic paradox of *Monarchia* is also operative, if far more effectively submerged, in *Commedia.* Dante's

political agenda requires that the temporal empire have a necessary and autonomous authority over the human will which, if properly exercised, would lead to the ideal condition of earthly peace and justice imagined in *Monarchia* book 1 and, fugitively and negatively, in *Purgatorio* 16 itself. The fallenness of the will, however, is the stumbling block that makes such a political utopia unrealizable, as Augustine had recognized long before in the *De civitate Dei*" (174). Ascoli's overall aim in his essay is to redefine the ways in which the *opere minori* of Dante can and should be read—to the point of inquiring what it means to think of such uniquely ambitious intellectual projects as *Convivio, De vulgari eloquentia,* and *Monarchia* as minor works and as pendants from the colossal achievement of the *Commedia.* At the core of his analysis is the "palinode," which, according to Ascoli, is Dante's most powerful rhetorical device. Albert Russell Ascoli, "Palinode and History in the Oeuvre of Dante," in *Dante Now: Current Trends in Dante Studies,* ed. Theodore J. Cachey, Jr. and Christian Moevs. (South Bend, IN: University of Notre Dame Press, 1995), 155-86. Donna Mancusi-Ungaro, in *Dante and the Empire,* also discusses the "strong similarities between the *Monarchia* and the *Commedia*" (15). The author states that while the "standard critical interpretations [of the two works] acknowledge that political justice and a well-ordered civil life remained equally as important to Dante's understanding of the universe as his faith in divine providence, they insist that the temporary solutions of the political treatise were ultimately contradicted and surpassed by the *Comedy*" (14). In contrast to this point of view, Mancusi-Ungaro argues that "the *Monarchia's* belief in the autonomy of the two powers and the ability of the temporal authority to lead [people] to happiness is redirected in the poem where the ideal of a renewed Church is realized and where the spiritual power is shown to dominate the secular even on earth. . . . The concerns of the *Monarchy* are human reason, social order, and imperialism, while the concerns of the poem are these as well as faith, eternal order and Christianity" (14, 15). In brief, the only difference between the *Monarchia* and the *Commedia,* it is argued, is one of genre.

20. *De Monarchia,* bk. 3, ch. 15, 77. As Charles Till Davis notes, "the greatest empire, or 'humana civilitas,' embraces the whole human family, and reaches its political fulfillment under the empire. That empire, or rule over the entire world, comes directly through God, not through any other authority such as the pope's jurisdiction. The papal dignity is even higher than the imperial, but exists in an entirely different sphere. The emperor relies on philosophical teachings to lead [human beings] to their human goal of temporal happiness; the pope relies on theological teachings to

lead them to their divine goal of salvation" (68). Davis correctly points out that "Dante never said that polity was twofold, since he could not envisage collaboration between emperor and pope in governing the [temporal world]: he thought the emperor should perform this task alone. At the same time, he did not think that the pope's position and function was dependent on the emperor's any more than the emperor's was dependent on the pope's" (77). "Dante and the Empire," in *The Cambridge Companion to Dante,* ed. Rachael Jacoff. (Cambridge: Cambridge University Press, 1993), 67-79.

21. Etienne Gilson, "Dante's Place in History," 125-26. Ernst H. Kantorowicz argues that Dante did make a complete break with the medieval view. As he puts it: "Dante's metaphysical surgery exceeded that of others who before him had separated the empire from the embrace of the church . . . by appropriating, as it were, the intellect for the state and leaving the care of the soul to the church. Dante did not turn *humanitas* against *Christianitas,* but thoroughly separated the one from the other; he took the 'human' out of the Christian compound and isolated it as a value in its own right." *The King's Two Bodies* (Princeton: Princeton University Press, 1957), 465.

22. Gilson, "Dante's Place in History," 132.

23. *De Monarchia,* bk. 3, ch. 16, 79-80.

24. Marjorie Reeves, "Marsiglio of Padua and Dante Alighieri," in *Trends in Medieval Political Thought,* ed. Beryl Smalley. (Oxford: Basil Blackwell, 1965), 92. Dino Bigongiari also comments that in Dante "the rule over human beings as they strive toward the fulfillment of their natural goals is assigned by God himself to the Emperor. . . . How is the Emperor selected? God selects the Emperor for He is the sole Elector: the so-called electors are merely mouthpieces of his Divine Providence. . . . We thus see that Dante in supporting his conviction of the necessity of a world-rule falls back upon the fiction of divine inspiration." "The Political Doctrine of Dante," in *Essays on Dante and Medieval Culture: Critical Studies of the Thought and Texts of Dante, St. Augustine, St. Thomas Aquinas, Marsilius of Padua, and other Medieval Subjects.* (Firenze: L. S. Olschki, 1964), 23.

25. Marsilius of Padua, *Defensor Pacis,* trans. and introd. Alan Gewirth, 2 vols. (New York: Columbia University Press, 1956), disc. 1, ch. 4, 2:13. Gewirth's extended introductory essay should be consulted for a comprehensive and insightful analysis of the *Defensor Pacis.*

26. *Defensor Pacis,* disc. 1, ch. 3, vol. 2:11-12.

27. *Defensor Pacis,* disc. 1, ch. 5, vol. 2:14.

28. *Defensor Pacis,* disc. 1, ch. 4, vol. 2:14.

29. *Defensor Pacis,* disc. 1, ch. 2, vol. 2:9. Cary J. Nederman analyzes a significant difference between Marsilius and Aristotle concerning the "public/private distinction and related matters." Nederman focuses on the extensive ramifications in Marsilius's thought of one major departure that he makes in his incorporation of Aristotle's ideas about the nature of a community. In contrast to Aristotle, the author argues, "Marsiglio of Padua explicitly denies to the family or household (*domus*) the status of a community. Instead, he repeatedly insists that the village is the 'first community.'" The author attempts to demonstrate that Marsilius's departure from his source is of considerable significance in the essential features of Marsilius's political thought. As the author puts it, "it is my argument that, by concentrating upon the circumstances of the household in the *Defensor,* we may discover how its non-communal conception of the family shapes its insistence upon individual choice and consent as the central feature of citizenship. . . . [Among other things], the private and willful qualities of the household contrast markedly with the basic principles of communal life described by the *Defensor*" (701, 705). "Private Will, Public Justice: Household, Community and Consent in Marsiglio of Padua's *Defensor Pacis,*" *Western Political Quarterly* (December 1990): 669-717. Also, by the same author, "Knowledge, Consent and the Critique of Political Representation in Marsiglio of Padua's *Defensor Pacis,*" *Political Studies* 1 (March 1991): 19-35. Here Nederman states that the *Defensor Pacis* contains a "sustained critique of crucial features of the theory and practice of political representation." It is argued that for Marsilius "the community is the final and indispensable determinant of its own welfare as manifested by law. When the *populus* enacts a statute, there is no question of its benefit to all citizens. No such certainty exists, however, when some grouping of lesser proportions than the whole community institutes law. This doctrine forms the basis for the *Defensor's* famed emphasis upon consent as the touchstone of good law and legitimate government. In stating that 'a law would be better observed by citizens anywhere when each one is seen to impose it on [themself],' Marsiglio expresses the apparent conviction that individual agreement to or acceptance of legislation is the only model of statutory enactment consistent with a properly ordered society," 19, 27-28.

30. *Defensor Pacis,* disc. 1, ch. 5, vol. 2:16.

31. Reeves, "Marsiglio of Padua and Dante Alighiere," 93.

32. A recent study of the notions of "corporatism" and "organicism" found in the *Defensor Pacis,* which focuses on "highlighting rather than minimizing the text's inconsistencies in an effort to probe Marsilius's underly-

ing ambivalencies toward diversity and unity," proposes that the major problem for Marsilius in his analysis of the causes of discord is the nature of diversity among people. As the author puts it: "The degree to which the state should have the right to suppress difference is problematic. . . . At every level of human association, from the family to the state, the whole, which maintains peace and tranquillity, is both dependent upon and threatened by the separate identities of its constituent parts. This dialectic between parts and whole forms the central problem on which Marsilius meditates. He arrives ultimately at several widely divergent solutions, which take the form of different images of unity and diversity in the state." The author points out that Marsilius uses the language of corporatism, which emphasizes the importance of trade guilds in communal society. At the same time, another language he employs for unity is that of biology, specifically, that of the body. It is claimed that Marsilius's recourse to the language of organicism betrays a lack of confidence in corporatist unity alone and a desire to impose upon it some more "natural" quality of unity. Renee P. Baernstein, "Corporatism and Organicism in Discourse I of Marsilius of Padua's *Defensor Pacis*," *Journal of Medieval and Early Modern Studies* 1 (Winter 1996): 113-38. See also Reeves, "Marsiglio of Padua and Dante Alighiere," 93-95; Nederman, "Private Will, Public Justice: Household, Community and Consent in Marsiglio of Padua's *Defensor Pacis*," 705-707.

33. Nederman, "Private Will, Public Justice: Household, Community and Consent in Marsiglio of Padua's *Defensor Pacis*," 707.

34. *Defensor Pacis*, disc. 1, ch. 19, vol. 2:90.

35. *Defensor Pacis*, disc. 3, ch. 3, vol. 2:431.

36. Marsilius does not categorically deny that there is a state of eternal bliss but rather that its existence, or the "means thereto," cannot be proven by rational means. The link between the temporal and the divine, in other words, is solely a matter of faith and has nothing to do with natural reason. The idea of some relationship between divine providence and the order of the temporal world is a complex issue in the *Defensor Pacis*. For a discussion of this point see Gewirth, *Defensor Pacis*, vol. 2:xlvi-lxv. Also, Reeves, "Marsiglio of Padua and Dante Alighiere," 100-104.

37. See Gewirth, *Defensor Pacis*, vol. 2:lxxiv.

38. *Defensor Pacis*, disc. 1, ch. 15, vol. 2:67.

39. See Gewirth, *Defensor Pacis*, vol. 2:lxxv.

40. Reeves, "Marsiglio of Padua and Dante Alighiere," 102.

41. *Defensor Pacis*, disc. 1, ch. 12, vol. 2:44.

42. See Gewirth, *Defensor Pacis*, vol. 2:lv.

Chapter 4
Reshaping Order: Thomas More's *Utopia*

An earlier version of this chapter appeared as "Temporal and Cosmic Order: The Making of a New Vision in Thomas More's *Utopia*," in *Proceedings of the International Conference on Patristic, Medieval, and Renaissance Studies* 8 (1984): 103-16.

1. Some critics regard the *Utopia* as a mere imitation of Plato's *Republic,* while others find that it is the result of a profound insight into the social evils and economic tendencies of More's age. For some commentators *Utopia* proposes social and political reforms that have actually been carried into practice, while others claim it has had no influence on social practice or political theory. From one point of view the work is said to describe in detail the life led by a community in an "ideal" commonwealth, from another it presents a picture of a "detestable" state. The ideological interpretations of the text include the "Christian," the "Marxist," and the "revolutionary" explanations. The following works should be consulted for an extended discussion of these various approaches to the study of the *Utopia*: Craig R. Thompson, "The Humanism of More Reappraised," *Thought* 52 (1977): 231-48; L. B. Liljegren, *Studies on the Origin and Early Tradition of English Utopian Fiction* (Copenhagen: Uppsala University Press, 1961), 15-81; Robert C. Elliott, *The Shape of Utopia: Studies in a Literary Genre* (Chicago: University of Chicago Press, 1970), 25-29; Joyce O. Hertzler, *The History of Utopian Thought* (New York: Macmillan, 1926), 59-78; J. H. Hexter and Edward Surtz, *Utopia,* in *The Complete Works of St. Thomas More* (New Haven: Yale University Press, 1965), vol. 4:xv-clxxxi; Raymond Ruyer, *L'Utopie et les utopies* (Paris: Presses Universitaires de France, 1950); William Nelson, ed., *Twentieth Century Interpretations of Utopia* (Englewood Cliffs, NJ: Prentice-Hall, 1968); Russell Ames, *Citizen Thomas More and His Utopia* (Princeton, NJ: Princeton University Press, 1949); J. H. Hexter. *More's Utopia: The Biography of an Idea* (Princeton, NJ: Princeton University Press, 1952); Edward Surtz, *The Praise of Pleasure: Philosophy, Education, and Communism in More's Utopia* (Cambridge, MA: Harvard University Press, 1957); Edward Surtz, *The Praise of Wisdom: A Commentary on the Religious and Moral Problems and Backgrounds of St. Thomas More's Utopia* (Chicago: Loyola University Press, 1957); Karl Mannheim, *Ideology and Utopia: An Intro-*

duction to the Sociology of Knowledge, trans. Louis Wirth and Edward Shils (New York: Harcourt Brace, 1940).

Several critics have commented on the important question concerning the influence of Augustine's *De civitate Dei* on More's *Utopia.* For Logan "the connections are neither numerous nor specific"; for Surtz, the influence is "general and tenuous"; and for Raitiere, "More got from Augustine no particular social or political doctrine, . . . but rather a feeling for the inevitable mingling of the good and bad in any social or legal order." See George M. Logan, *The Meaning of More's* Utopia (Princeton, NJ: Princeton University Press, 1983), 192 n.; Edward J. Surtz, *The Complete Works of St. Thomas More,* vol. 4: *Utopia,* ed. Edward Surtz, S. J. and J. H. Hexter (New Haven, CT: Yale University Press, 1965), clxvi-clxvii; Martin N. Raitiere, "More's *Utopia* and *The City of God,*" *Studies in the Renaissance,* 20 (1973): 164. A recent study offers an insightful and detailed analysis, and contrary point of view, on this topic that should be consulted. Wegemer argues that in the *Utopia* "Augustine is present just as Plato and Cicero are present—through allusion. . . . More carefully creates a pattern of Augustinian allusions—a subtext if you will, thus providing an internal measure by which we are invited to rethink the perennial issues regarding the best way of life and the best form of the republic. These pervasive Augustinian allusions also provide a measure by which we can judge the fictional regime that Raphael presents, revealing in the process a level of Lucianic comedy previously unnoticed." Gerald Wegemer, *"The City of God* in Thomas More's *Utopia,"* *Renascence* 66 (Winter 1992): 117.

On one of the other major focuses of scholarship concerning the *Utopia,* namely, whether the *Utopia* was written in imitation of Plato's *Republic,* two sharply divergent opinions are provided by White and Starnes. White agrees that there is some truth to the claim that More wrote his work in imitation of the *Republic,* but he sees this, for the most part, as a misleading statement. He argues that the assertion of imitation fails to recognize More's overall use of classical philosophy. As he puts it, *"Utopia* is not simply an excursus into the problems of councilorship and a critique of sixteenth-century Europe, but is, more importantly, More's testimony of the moral, social and political utility of classical philosophy." Thomas I. White, "Pride and the Public Good: Thomas More's Use of Plato in *Utopia," Journal of the History of Philosophy* 4 (1982): 330. In contrast, Starnes claims that "the *Utopia* is the *Republic* recast in a new mould applicable to the demands of contemporary Christianity as these were understood by More. . . . In a word, it is a Christianized *Republic."* Starnes seems to modify this view in his later statement where he says that it is their "*implicit* Christianity that prevents the Utopians from simply falling back into the social and political solutions of antiquity, while at the same time it in no way makes their solution dependent on any special revelation or a belief that is the possession of some but not all." Colin Starnes, *The New Republic* (Waterloo, Ont.: Wilfrid Laurier University Press, 1990), 3, 102 (emphasis in original). See also, Nicholas Opanasets, "More Platonism," *The Review of Politics* (Summer 1989): 412-34.

2. See Henri Frankfort, et al., *Before Philosophy: The Intellectual Adventure of Ancient Man* (Baltimore, MD: Penguin, 1949), 11-19; 237-44. Ugo Bianchi has also noted that the general pattern of the theogonic poems of archaic Greece "were based on the concept that the gods and the universe as they actually stand had been put into existence as a consequence of an innate movement upwards starting from some primordial, elementary foundations and ending in the actual situation of stability and order." See "The Ideal Foundations of Greek Cosmogonical Thought," in *Mythology and Cosmic Order,* ed. Rene Gothoni and Juha Pentikainen (Helsinki: Suomalaisen Kirjallisuuden Seura, 1987), 9.

3. For a discussion of the influence of Hebrew thought on the transition from Egyptian and Mesopotamian thinking to that of the Greek period consult Frankfort, et al., *Before Philosophy,* 241-48.

4. Although the usual translation of *polis* is "state," there was in Greek thought no distinction made between society and state. We note that for Aquinas, writing in the thirteenth century, human beings are "social and political animals," but in Aristotle's view, whose thought Aquinas had assimilated, human beings are only "political animals." For both Aristotle and Plato, all social life is political life; the state includes within itself the entire collective activity of its members. As Charles McIlwain puts it, in Greek thought "the *polis* is coterminous with society." *The Growth of Political Thought in the West: From the Greeks to the End of the Middle Ages* (New York: Macmillan Company, 1932), 5. And according to Harry Jaffa, the central characteristic of the political community or *polis* for Aristotle is that "it is the community that includes all other human communities, while itself being included by none." "Aristotle," in *History of Political Philosophy*, ed. Leo Strauss and Joseph Cropsey (Chicago: Rand McNally, 1972), 65. In sum, for Greek thinkers, the term *polis* refers to an all-inclusive entity and it implies an organic relationship among the various kinds of associations people form within the community.

5. It was this perspective, the notion of the state as a natural entity with its own operating principles, and as according to human nature, that gave rise to a mode of thought that dealt solely with the idea of the right order of society—

political philosophy. As George Sabine and others have observed, the Greeks were the first to view society as a coherent, interconnected whole; a "system" of interrelated functions, an ordered structure, a political society. Sabine points out that political and social questions and isolated political ideas were matters of common knowledge and preceded the appearance of explicit political theory. But, "the personal agency by which suggestive ideas were turned into explicit philosophy was Socrates." *A History of Political Theory* (New York: Holt, Rinehart and Winston, 1961), 32. For further discussion see Sabine, ch. 2, 21-34; Sheldon S. Wolin, *Politics and Vision: Continuity and Innovation in Western Political Thought* (Boston: Little Brown, 1960), ch. 2, 28-34. Also, as noted in the introduction, see Ernan McMullin, "Cosmic Order in Plato and Aristotle," in *The Concept of Order*, ed. Paul G. Kuntz (Washington: University of Washington Press, 1968); Ernest Barker, *Greek Political Theory: Plato and His Predecessors* (New York: Barnes & Noble, 1918); Strauss and Cropsey, ed. *History of Political Philosophy*; McIlwain, *The Growth of Political Thought in the West.*

6. A. J. Carlyle, "St. Augustine and *The City of God,*" in *The Social and Political Ideas of Some Great Mediaeval Thinkers,* ed. F. J. C. Hearnshaw (New York: Barnes & Noble, 1928), 45.

7. See Carlyle, "St. Augustine and *The City of God,*" 44; Sabine, *A History of Political Theory,* 148-51.

8. Since for Aquinas too the whole of the natural order is subject to the order of divine grace, from this point of view, as Fortin puts it, "the simply best regime is not, as it was for Aristotle, the work of [human beings] or of practical reason guided by philosophy." Ernest L. Fortin, "St. Thomas Aquinas," in Strauss and Cropsey, ed. *History of Political Philosophy,* 233.

9. There are several sources that deal with the subject of relative and absolute natural law. A particularly good treatment is in Otto Gierke, *Natural Law and the Theory of Society: 1500 to 1800,* trans. and introd. Ernest Barker (Boston: Beacon Press, 1957; first published by Cambridge University press in two volumes in 1934), xxxiv-xl; also, A. P. D'Entréves, *The Notion of the State* (London: Oxford University Press, 1967), pt. 3, ch. 2, 161-69. And, an excellent collection of essays on the history of natural law theory can be found in Harold J. Johnson, ed. *The Medieval Tradition of Natural Law* (Kalamazoo, MI: Western Michigan University Press, 1987).

10. *Utopia,* in *The Complete Works of St. Thomas More,* ed. Edward Surtz, S. J. and J. H. Hexter. vol. 4 (New Haven, CT: Yale University Press, 1965), 183.

11. *Utopia,* 161. The problem of understanding More's treatment of the relationship between faith and reason stems in large part from his argument

here that reason supplements faith by affirming certain fundamental religious truths. A consideration central to an interpretation of this issue is More's general assessment of human nature. While More, like Aquinas, regards humankind as fallen he nonetheless argues that we are by nature capable of making autonomous choices based upon what reason concludes will most benefit us individually and, in turn, society in general. As Timothy Kenyon says, "it must constantly be borne in mind that More oscillated between two positions—on the one hand, the admission that we are incapable of absolutely autonomous or self-determining moral action, and, on the other hand, the conviction that despite this limitation we would be held responsible *as if* we were capable of such conduct. In this lies the basis of More's conception of responsibility, an understanding which in turn informs his appreciation of freedom of choice." *Utopian Communism and Political Thought in Early Modern England* (London: Pinter Publishers, 1989), 112. In commenting on More's purpose in the *Utopia,* Kenyon argues that "More's assessment of the depravity of human nature informs his belief that individuals might be capable of correct behavior on a sustained basis only as members of a society in which conduct is precisely regulated by institutional means. His advocacy of communism is but one aspect of this line of thought. And this reasoning extends to his views on the state," 113.

12. *Utopia,* 217.

13. *Utopia,* 161.

14. *Utopia,* 163.

15. *Utopia,* 217.

16. When we examine the general structure and the details of the *Utopia* as a study of order we find a pattern throughout the work that is consistent with an "ordering vision." That is, all concepts of order look at order "whole," they have as their purpose the structured and systematic arrangement of "things," and they relate these phenomena to the ends for which the various entities have been arranged. From the point of view of order it is not surprising, then, to find that More looks at order whole or complete, that he systematically arranges diverse things, and that he relates the various "parts" of his scheme of order to the ends for which they have been arranged. See the discussion in the introduction that deals with the general characteristics of the concept of order.

17. *Utopia,* 113.

18. *Utopia,* 113.

19. *Utopia,* 117.

20. See note 16 above.

21. *Utopia,* 117.
22. *Utopia,* 119-21.
23. See note 16 above.
24. Plato, *Laws,* trans. A. E. Taylor, in *The Collected Dialogues of Plato,* ed. E. Hamilton and H. Cairns (New York: Bollingen Foundation, 1961), Law 6, 1333-48. For a brief but useful discussion of Plato's ideas in the *Laws* that a more harmonious political order could be created by transferring the properties of numbers to society see Wolin, *Politics and Vision,* 49-50.
25. *Utopia,* 135-37.
26. As many critics have noted, the words "syphogrant" and "tranibor" have no meaning beyond the way they are used by More in the *Utopia,* namely, words used at titles for public officials.
27. Plato, *Republic,* trans. Paul Shorey, in *The Collected Dialogues of Plato,* ed. Hamilton and Cairns. Plato puts it this way: "The origin of the city [that is, the state] . . . is to be found in the fact that we do not severally suffice for our own needs, but each of us lacks many things. . . . We, being in need of many things, gather many into one place . . . and to this dwelling we give the name city or state," 2.369b:615.
28. *Aristotle's Politics,* trans. B. Jowett, introd. H. W. C. Davis (London: Oxford University Press, 1931). According to Aristotle, since "the earlier forms of society are natural, so is the state, for it is the end of them, and the completed nature is the end," 1.2:28.
29. Augustine, *De civitate Dei,* trans. George L. McCracken, et al. (Cambridge, MA: Harvard University Press, 1957-1972), Loeb Classical Library, 7 vols. Throughout the text Augustine makes several references to the idea that human beings are by nature social beings. For example, in bk. 12, ch. 28 he says that "there is nothing so . . . sociable in its true nature . . . as the human race" 4.129. Later, in bk. 19, ch. 5 where he talks about the nature of the citizens of the *civitas Dei,* he says, "How could the City of God . . . begin at the start or progress in its course or reach its appointed goal, if the life of the saints were not social?" 6.139.
30. In Augustine's view, if God had not created the state, anarchy would reign and people would destroy each other because of their propensity toward "love of self" rather than "love of God." The corrective to this inevitability is a state conceived of as a remedial instrument which is itself part of God's divine plan. For Augustine, the "ideal" temporal state is that state which permits the citizens of the *civitas Dei* to pursue salvation without political interference. "As far as this moral life is concerned, which is passed and ended in a few days, what difference does it make . . . under

which ruler [we] live, if only the rulers do not force [us] to commit unholy and unjust deeds." *De civitate Dei,* 2.219; 5.17.

31. Walter Ullmann, *A History of Political Thought: The Middle Ages* (Baltimore: Penguin Books, 1965), 179.

32. As we have seen, Aquinas's thought was greatly influenced by the Aristotelian revival of the twelfth century. And one of the leading ideas that Aquinas derives from Aristotle is the view that human beings are by nature political animals. According to Aquinas, if we were by nature solitary animals, the order of reason and that of divine law would have been sufficient. But since we are social and political animals a third order, that is, political authority, is required whereby we are directed in relation to others among whom we must live. As a product of nature and as a necessary means, the authority or power of government in general has its own basically natural mode of operation in its pursuit of aims finalistically inherent in the nature of human beings.

33. The idea of "membership" in Greek, Stoic, and Augustinian thought is a complex subject. Very briefly, we have seen that as used by Augustine the term *civitas terrena* does not refer to earthly political and social arrangements; rather, in Augustinian thought it is preordained that all human beings are members of either one or the other of two universal societies—the *civitas Dei* or the *civitas terrena.* Like the Stoics, and unlike Plato and Aristotle, Augustine proposes that we share dual membership; on the one hand, we are members of a natural universal society, and on the other we are members of a conventional temporal state. The Stoics had substituted for the earlier Greek notion of membership in a single *polis* the concept of dual membership—one universal, the other temporal. This concept of dual membership, as we have seen, greatly influenced Augustine's thinking. On the notion of dualism in Stoic philosophy and its relation to the idea of membership consult Michael Lapidge, "Stoic Cosmology," in *The Stoics,* ed. J. M. Rist (Berkeley: University of California Press, 1987), 161-85; G. Verbeke, *Stoicism in Medieval Thought* (Washington: Catholic University of America Press, 1983), 21-44; J. M. Rist, *Stoic Philosophy* (London: Cambridge University Press, 1969), 256-88; and Wolin, *Politics and Vision,* chs. On "Space and Community" and "Time and Community."

34. *De Monarchia,* bk. 3, ch. 16, 78.

35. *Defensor Pacis,* disc. 1, ch. 5, vol. 2:14.

36. *Aristotle's Politics,* trans. Jowett, 3.4:106.

37. Gierke, *Natural Law,* 35-36.

38. John Freeman, "More's Place in 'No Place': The Self-Fashioning Transaction in *Utopia,*" *Texas Studies in Literature and Language* 2 (Summer 1992): 210.

39. As we have seen, Christian thinkers in the Middle Ages, while commonly distinguishing philosophical from theological truths, part company on which truths are assigned to the sectors of reason and faith. For Aquinas the existence of God is rationally demonstrable. In contrast, Duns Scotus holds that not all of God's essential attributes are analytically accessible; such perfections as omnipotence, immensity, omnipresence, justice, and mercy are certainly known only through revelation. William of Ockham further reduces the compass of a rational understanding of God, arguing that we cannot analytically establish with certitude even the existence of God. In contrast to this two-storied approach to reality, More, in the *Utopia*, restricts knowledge to the rational level alone. Bracketing or prescinding from the truths of Christianity More proposes a religion in Utopia founded not on revelation at all but on philosophy and reason. And, as More includes nothing of the strictly supernatural in the religious outlook of Utopia, so he recognizes no influence, as we have seen, of the supernatural in the shaping of order in the temporal realm. For a discussion of William of Ockham's ideas on this topic see Frederick Copleston, *Ockham to Suarez*, vol. 3 of *A History of Philosophy* (Westminster, MD: Newman Press, 1953), 80-85. Also see note 11 above.

Chapter 5
Order and Progress: Francis Bacon's *New Atlantis*

1. More tells us that the Utopians "explore the secrets of nature," that they are expert "in the courses of the stars and the movements of the celestial bodies," and that they are able to "forecast rains, winds, and all the other changes in weather by definite signs." But the Utopians do not formulate any new theories about nature or about the nature of human beings: "As to the causes of all these phenomena, . . . and, in fine, of the origin and nature of the heavens and the universe, they partly treat of them in the same way as our ancient philosophers and, as the latter differ from one another they, too, partly, in introducing new theories, disagree with them all and yet do not in all respects agree with fellow Utopians." The point is that More does not go on to explain which of the ancient theories of nature the Utopians accept nor does he discuss the new theories they have introduced. *Utopia*, in *The Complete Works of St. Thomas More*, ed. Edward Surtz, S. J. and J. H. Hexter, vol. 4 (New Haven, CT: Yale University Press, 1965), 183, 159, 161.

2. It is generally agreed that the decisive break with scholastic and medieval thought took place in the seventeenth century. It is in this period that we find the rise of the "scientific" explanation of reality and the decline of Aristotelian and scholastic conceptions of knowledge. Basil Willey has summarized the new attitude this way: "It was in the seventeenth century that modern European thought seems to have assumed, once more, that its appointed task was *La Recherche de la Vérité,* the discovery and declaration, according to its lights, of the True Nature of Things." *The Seventeenth Century Background* (New York: Columbia University Press, 1965), 1. The distinguishing characteristic of the seventeenth century was its emphasis on the investigation and interpretation of the phenomena and events of nature. It was a new way of thinking which emphasized physics rather than metaphysics, efficient causes rather than final causes, and natural knowledge rather than supernatural knowledge. Given this change in outlook, a point of view that resulted in a fundamental revaluation of our place in the scheme of the universe, it is not surprising that we should find in this period a new notion of order and new ideas about human reason and the state. In sum, in the seventeenth century there was an entirely different starting-point that resulted in the formulation of completely new explanations.

3. It is not my purpose here to examine the range of Bacon's thought regarding the classification of all knowledge on the psychological basis of memory, imagination, and reason, but to focus attention on his emphasis upon a sharp demarcation between the truths of faith and reason. Bacon's ideas on the classification of knowledge are most fully developed in *The Advancement of Learning* and the *De Augmentis.* Among others who offer a critical assessment of Bacon's thought see Benjamin Farrington, *The Philosophy of Francis Bacon* (Chicago: University of Chicago Press, 1966); J. G. Crowther, *Francis Bacon: The First Statesman of Science* (London: Cresset Press, 1960); Brian Vickers, ed. *Essential Articles for the Study of Francis Bacon* (Hamden, CT: Archon Books, 1968); Paolo Rossi, *Francis Bacon from Magic to Science,* trans. Sacha Rubinovitch (Chicago: University of Chicago Press, 1968); Karl R. Wallace, *Francis Bacon on the Nature of Man* (Urbana: University of Illinois Press, 1967). Also, for studies with a focus on Bacon's political philosophy see Howard B. White, *Peace Among the Willows: the Political Philosophy of Francis Bacon* (The Hague: Martinus Nijhoff, 1968); John E. Leary, *Francis Bacon and the Politics of Science* (Ames: Iowa State University Press, 1994); Charles Whitney, *Francis Bacon and Modernity* (New Haven, CT: Yale University Press, 1986).

4. Francis Bacon, *The Advancement of Learning,* in *The Works of Francis Bacon,* ed. James Spedding, Robert Leslie Ellis, and Douglas Denon Heath, 15 vols. (Boston: Brown and Taggard, 1860-64), bk. 1, vol. 6:95-96; hereafter cited as *Works.*

5. *The Advancement of Learning,* in *Works,* bk. 3, vol. 8:478.

6. In his insistence on the bounds of reason, Bacon does not deny the legitimacy of faith. On the contrary, an awareness of the limits of the human intellect demonstrates the need for faith. Thus, while we learn nothing about divine providence through natural science, the investigation of nature leads ultimately to an acknowledgment of God. As Bacon puts it: "It is an assured truth and a conclusion of experience, that a little or superficial knowledge of philosophy may incline the mind to atheism, but a farther proceeding therein doth bring the mind back again to religion; for in the entrance of philosophy, when the second causes, which are next unto the senses, do offer themselves to the mind, if it dwell and stay there, it may induce some oblivion, of the highest cause; but when a [person] passeth on farther, and seeth the dependence of causes and the works of Providence, then . . . we easily believe that the highest link of nature's chain must needs be tied to the foot of Jupiter's chair." *The Advancement of Learning,* in *Works,* bk. 1, vol. 6:96-97.

7. *De Augmentis,* in *Works,* bk. 9, vol. 9:345, 347.

8. *The Advancement of Learning,* in *Works,* bk. 3, vol. 8:477.

9. S. L. Bethell, *The Cultural Revolution of the Seventeenth Century* (London: Dennis Dobson, 1951), 63-64.

10. Stephen L. Collins, *From Divine Cosmos to Sovereign State: An Intellectual History of Consciousness and the Idea of Order in Renaissance England* (New York: Oxford University Press, 1989), 144.

11. As Basil Willey puts it: "Bacon's desire to separate religious truth and scientific truth was in the interests of science, not of religion. He wished to *keep science pure from religion;* the opposite part of the process—keeping religion pure from science—did not interest him nearly so much. What he harps on is always how science has been hampered at every stage by the prejudice and conservatism of theologians. . . . Religious truth, then, must be 'skied,' elevated far out of reach, not in order that it may be more devoutly approached, but in order to keep it out of mischief." *The Seventeenth Century Background,* 29; emphasis in original.

12. *New Atlantis,* in *Works,* vol. 5:398.

13. *Novum Organum,* in *Works,* Aphorism XXXVI, vol. 8:75.

14. *Novum Organum,* in *Works,* Aphorism XXXI, vol. 8:74.

15. Collins, *Divine Cosmos,* 145.

16. See "To the Reader," *New Atlantis,* in *Works,* vol. 5:357.

17. Although the size is different, Bacon, like More, makes the patriarchal family the basic political unit. Bacon too has the authority of the patriarchal head, the Tirsan, supported by public officials. The major celebration in the *New Atlantis,* called the Feast of the Family, is "done at the expense of the state" and it culminates in a contract between the extended family and the state symbolized by the presentation of a scroll to the Father of the Family. At the conclusion of the celebration, "the herald, with three curtesies, or rather inclinations, cometh up as far as the half-pace; and there first taketh into his hand the scroll. This scroll is the King's Charter, containing gift of revenue, and many privileges, exemptions, and points of honor, granted to the Father of the Family." *Works,* vol. 5:388. The significance here is the public presentation and celebration of a formal contract between the state and the family in which it is agreed that the state will assist the Tirsan, if necessary, in carrying out his decrees and orders. "The governor assisteth, to the end to put in execution by his public authority the decrees and orders of the Tirsan." *Works,* vol. 5:386.

18. *Novum Organum,* in *Works,* Aphorism LXXXI, vol. 8:113.

19. Whitney, *Francis Bacon and Modernity,* 19.

20. *New Atlantis,* in *Works,* vol. 5:368.

21. *New Atlantis,* in *Works,* vol. 5:368.

22. *New Atlantis,* in *Works,* vol. 5:386.

23. *New Atlantis,* in *Works,* vol. 5:411. Several critics have commented on the ambiguity inherent in the Fellows' oath of secrecy. For example, one asks whether "such regulation is a result of the belief that knowledge is power and must be held by the elite or the idea that new knowledge simply poses a threat to a static social order based upon custom—that is left unclear. What is equally important about this brief passage—though, again, tantalizing rather than really explanatory—is the fact that the members of Salomon's House have it in their power to withhold knowledge even from the state. At the very least this provision suggests a certain autonomy of the scientific community vis-à-vis the political authorities. Whether it should be taken to mean that in any vital respects the scientific establishment was in fact superior to the civil government is an open question." John Leary, *Francis Bacon and the Politics of Science,* 253-54. In contrast, Faulkner looks at the work's theme of secrecy as a rhetorical devise used by Bacon to conceal the radical ideas he presents in the *New Atlantis.* "The secretive handling of matters of government is obvious in the *New Atlantis,* for it is not only tacit but also explicit and even a thematic policy of Bensalem. . . . One may suppose the *New Atlantis's* peculiar mixture of revelation and concealment, of political comprehensiveness in an extraor-

dinary way mixed with political indefiniteness in many ordinary ways, is calculated to serve a function. I suggest that it is a rhetorical function. *New Atlantis* is calculatedly visionary. It proclaims a science to save humanity at large, and, in effect, it proclaims the duty to found a scientific civilization. Precisely for the sake of such a cosmopolitan aim, it appeals above governments and above the most controversial political differences within nations and among nations. It abstracts from controversies over forms of rule. . . . *New Atlantis* parades the scientific and economic improvement to come, while it veils the divisions and revolutions, in morals, politics, and religion, also to be undergone. But it also indicates what it veils, for those who need to know what they're getting into." Robert K. Faulkner, *Francis Bacon and the Project of Progress* (Lanham, MD: Rowman & Littlefield, 1993), 235-36. And from yet another perspective the subversive nature of Bacon's challenge to the status quo is seen as restricted by his insistence on method and classification. He also conceals his radical purpose by showing the "workings of new knowledge in the service of traditional paternal authority." See Sharon Achinstein, "How to be a Progressive Without Looking Like One: History and Knowledge in Bacon's *New Atlantis*," *CLIO* 17 (Spring 1988): 250, 251.

24. Faulkner, *Francis Bacon and the Project of Progress,* 255.

25. Faulkner, 256.

26. Denise Albanese, *New Science, New World* (Durham: Duke University Press, 1996), 107-108; 113-14.

27. *Novum Organum,* in *Works,* Aphorism XCIX, vol. 8:135.

28. Another topic related to Bacon's attitude toward nature that goes beyond the scope of this study but which forms a part of his overall philosophy of nature is his view of the doctrine of decay. Victor Harris points out that "in the work of Francis Bacon we find expressed the one idea which, perhaps more than any other, is to render untenable the doctrine of decay. . . . The great change which finally disposes of it is the separation of the whole world into its disparate parts; the new emphasis upon the secular, natural world, the discovery in nature of an order which does not have human beings for its center, its climax, and its little world." *All Coherence Gone* (Chicago: University of Chicago Press, 1949), 130. Harris presents an insightful treatment of the doctrine of decay in sixteenth and seventeenth century thought.

29. *Novum Organum,* in *Works,* Aphorism X, vol. 8:69.

30. *Novum Organum,* in *Works,* Aphorism III, vol. 8:67-68.

31. *Parasceve,* in *Works,* Aphorism I, vol. 8:357.

32. *Novum Organum,* in *Works,* Aphorism XLVIII, vol. 8:81.

33. *De Sapientia Veterum,* in *Works,* Aphorism XXVI, vol. 13:147.
34. White, *Peace Among the Willows,* 15. In addition to his study of Bacon's political thought, White also develops a thoughtful analysis of Bacon's use of symbolism in the *New Atlantis.*
35. *Magna Instauratio,* in *Works,* Preface, vol. 8:18.
36. Collins, *Divine Cosmos,* 145. Sidney Warhaft, on the other hand, although he does agree that Bacon's essential orientation was far more secular than sacral, claims that much of Bacon's thought is fundamentally influenced by his acceptance of two main affirmations of divine providence, namely, "that change or fortune does not really exist, and that there is an ultimate over-all order in creation. . . . Although Bacon tended to reject many of the ideas of degree . . . and of those correspondences between microcosm and macrocosm so dear to what has become known as the Elizabethan World Picture, he nonetheless insisted on the order of nature and on the continuance of that order, somewhat diminished but still discernible, after the fall." Warhaft concludes that while Bacon is "at times not far from Descartes, he could never have arrived at a *Cogitato,* for his understanding of the part providence plays in the world would not only have prevented him from excluding the role of the divine in nature and in the knowledge of nature, but would also have stopped him from making human beings as autonomous as Descartes does. Naturalistic though he strove to be, he was unable to ignore the supernaturalistic in his thought." See "The Providential Order in Bacon's New Philosophy," *Studies in the Literary Imagination* 4 (1971): 52, 53, 64.
37. *Novum Organum,* in *Works,* Aphorism XLV, vol. 8:79.
38. *Magna Instauratio,* in *Works,* Plan of the Work, vol. 8:53.
39. *Novum Organum,* in *Works,* Aphorism XXI, vol. 8:72.
40. *Novum Organum,* in *Works,* Aphorism XCIX, vol. 8:135-36.
41. *Novum Organum,* in *Works,* Second Book of Aphorisms, Aphorism X, vol. 8:178-79.
42. W. Donald Oliver, *Theory of Order* (Yellow Springs, OH: Antioch Press, 1951), 315.
43. Oliver, 316.
44. *Novum Organum,* in *Works,* Aphorism CV, vol. 8:138.
45. *Novum Organum,* in *Works,* Preface, vol. 8:60.
46. Collins, *Divine Cosmos,* 146.

Conclusion

1. For George Logan, "the modernity of *Utopia* can be accounted for in terms of More's humanism. This modernity has two elements. First, as is obvious to any twentieth-century reader, the Utopian construct includes a number of features that strikingly foreshadow the modern welfare state. Second, the book embodies, as we have seen, a distinctively modern approach to the analysis of social problems and their possible solutions." *The Meaning of More's* Utopia (Princeton, NJ: Princeton University Press, 1983), 259. Also, Krishan Kumar says: "In its universality and fundamental egalitarianism, in its recognition of the necessity and dignity of labour, Utopia reflects More's Christianity more than his classicism. . . . This is what also separates Utopia from all previous versions and visions of the good society. More's Utopia announced that the modern utopia would be democratic, not hierarchical." *Utopianism* (Minneapolis: University of Minnesota Press, 1991), 50.

2. J. H. Hexter, Introduction, *Utopia,* in *The Complete Works of St. Thomas More,* ed. Edward Surtz, S. J., and J. H. Hexter, vol. 4 (New Haven, CT: Yale University Press, 1965), cxii.

3. John G. Gunnell, *Political Theory: Tradition and Interpretation* (Cambridge, MA: Winthrop Publishers, 1979), 149. Gunnell correctly notes that "although theory as literature, the creation of a city in speech, may become in some respects a surrogate for political action and an actual political creation, it is not simply compensatory fantasy or merely neurotic displacement born of frustration in which the theorist plays out a dream as creator and manipulator," 147. In direct contrast to what some critics want to suggest, More's ideal commonwealth is clearly the framework for the presentation of a serious plan for social and political change.

4. Gunnell, 153.

5. Charles Whitney, *Francis Bacon and Modernity* (New Haven, CT: Yale University Press, 1986), 197. The question of Bacon's place in the history of the idea of progress is not relevant to this study, but it is worth mentioning that there is considerable disagreement on the issue. Whitney claims, for example, that while Bacon did not develop a doctrine of progress, "the essential grounds for hope discussed in *Novum Organum* I, 92-114 are that Bacon's own method of discovery provides a new basis for hope and progress, an opportunity to break out of the cycles of history," 47. In contrast, as Whitney also points out, Robert Nisbet "dismisses Bacon and most other Renaissance thinkers as relatively unimportant in the history of the idea," 48. For a general

discussion of the topic see J. B. Bury, *The Idea of Progress* (New York: Dover Publications, 1955; first published by Macmillan in 1932). In his excellent study on Bacon's thought, which includes a treatment of Bacon's utopianism, Jerry Weinberger proposes that an understanding of the modern age requires a critical awareness of the difference between naïve and realistic utopianism. Naïve utopianism, according to Weinberger, is the necessary hope of human beings as productive animals. Realistic utopianism is the "teaching about naïve utopianism that comes from thinking about human beings as political animals." From Bacon, Weinberger says, "we learn that the roots of the modern project are both realistically and naïvely utopian. Therefore, we should not think that our age is wholly new and not tied to a wisdom older than its founders. This latter fact is the source of possible moderate hope. . . . Perhaps it was because Bacon so deftly combined the new promise of freedom with the realistic knowledge of its limits that Rousseau, the only other modern realistic utopian, called him *le plus grand, peut-être, des Philosophes." Science, Faith, and Politics: Francis Bacon and the Utopian Roots of the Modern Age* (Ithaca, NY: Cornell University Press, 1985), 330-32.

6. Stephen L. Collins, *From Divine Cosmos to Sovereign State* (New York: Oxford University Press, 1989), 166.

7. Collins, 166.

8. Francis Bacon, *Magna Instauratio*, in *The Works of Francis Bacon*, ed. James Spedding, Robert Leslie Ellis, and Douglas Denon Heath, 15 vols. (Boston: Brown and Taggard, 1860-64), bk. 1, vol. 6:95-96.

9. For other approaches to the study of utopianism that are informed by post-structuralist theories of language, or by Ernst Bloch's notion of a "utopian impulse," which he designates as "anticipatory consciousness," or by the argument that utopia is rooted in discontent, or, finally, by an analysis of the significance of the dramatic shift in focus that is found in contemporary feminist utopianism, the following works should be consulted: Lucy Sargisson, *Contemporary Feminist Utopianism* (New York: Routledge, 1996); Ruth Levitas, *The Concept of Utopia* (Hemel Hempstead, Eng.: Philip Allan, 1990); Tom Moylan, *Demand the Impossible: Science Fiction and the Utopian Imagination* (New York: Methuen, 1986); Ernst Bloch, *The Principle of Hope*. 3 vols., trans. Neville Plaice, Stephen Plaice, and Paul Knight (Cambridge, MA: MIT Press, 1986; first published in 1957); and Darko Suvin, "Defining the Literary Genre of Utopia," *Studies in the Literary Imagination* 6 (Fall 1973): 121-45. For a discussion of the characteristics of and the influences that gave rise to modern dystopian literature see M. Keith Booker, *The Dystopian Impulse in Modern Literature* (Westport, CT: Greenwood Press, 1994).

Bibliography

Achinstein, Sharon. "How To Be A Progressive Without Looking Like One: History and Knowledge in Bacon's *New Atlantis.*" *CLIO: A Journal of Literature, History and the Philosophy of History* 17 (Spring 1988): 249-64.

Adams, Jeremy D. *The Populus of Augustine and Jerome: A Study in the Patristic Sense of Community.* New Haven, CT: Yale University Press, 1971.

Albanese, Denise. *New Science, New World.* Durham: Duke University Press, 1996.

Alighieri, Dante. *De Monarchia.* Translated by Herbert W. Schneider. Introduction by Dino Bigongiari. New York: Liberal Arts Press, 1949.

Ames, Russell. *Citizen Thomas More and His Utopia.* New Jersey: Princeton University Press, 1949.

Aquinas, Thomas. *Summa theologiae,* Blackfriars' edition and translation. New York: McGraw-Hill, 1964.

———. *The Basic Writings of Saint Thomas Aquinas.* Translated and with an introduction by Anton C. Pegis. 2 vols. New York: Random House, 1945.

Argyros, Alexander J. *A Blessed Rage for Order.* Ann Arbor: University of Michigan Press, 1991.

Aristotle. *Politics.* Translated by Benjamin Lowett. London: Oxford University Press, 1931.

Arnheim, Rudolph. *Entropy and Art: An Essay on Disorder and Order.* Berkeley: University of California Press, 1971.

Ascoli, Albert Russell. "Palinode and History in the Oeuvre of Dante." In *Dante Now: Current Trends in Dante Studies,* edited by Theodore J. Cachey, Jr., and Christian Moevs, 155-86. South Bend, IN: University of Notre Dame Press, 1995.

Aughterson, Kate. "The Waking Vision: Reference in the *New Atlantis.*" *Renaissance Quarterly* 1 (Spring 1992): 119-37.

Augustine, Aurelius. *De Civitate Dei.* Translated by George E. McCracken, W. M. Green, D. S. Wiesen, P. Levine, and E. M. Sanford. 7 vols. Loeb Classical Library. Cambridge: Harvard University Press, 1957-1972.

———. *The Retractations.* Translated by Mary I. Bogan. Washington: Catholic University Press, 1968.

Aurelius, Marcus. *Meditations.* In *The Stoic and Epicurean Philosophers,* edited by Whitney J. Oates. New York: Random House, 1940.

Bacon, Francis. *The Works of Francis Bacon.* Edited by James Spedding, Robert Leslie Ellis, and Douglas Denon Heath. 15 vols. Boston: Brown and Taggard, 1860-64.

Baernstein, P. Renee. "Corporatism and Organicism in Discourse I of Marsilius of Padua's *Defensor Pacis.*" *Journal of Medieval and Early Modern Studies* 1 (Winter 1996): 113-34.

Baker, David Weil. "Topical Utopias: Radicalizing Humanism in Sixteenth-Century England." *Studies in English Literature* 1 (Winter 1996): 1-30.

Barker, Ernest. *Greek Political Theory: Plato and His Predecessors.* New York: Barnes & Noble, 1918.

Barth, Hans. *The Idea of Order: Contributions to a Philosophy of Politics.* Holland: D. Reidel Publishing Company, 1960.

Baynes, Norman H. *The Political Ideas of St. Augustine's* De Civitate Dei. London: The Historical Association, 1936.

Bethell, S. L. *The Cultural Revolution of the Seventeenth Century.* London: Dennis Dobson, Ltd., 1951.

Bianchi, Ugo. "The Ideal Foundations of Greek Cosmogonical Thought." In *Mythology and Cosmic Order,* edited by Rene Gothoni, and Juha Pentikainen, 8-15. Helsinki: Suomalaisen Kirjallisuuden Seura, 1987.

Bigongiari, Dino. *Essays on Dante and Medieval Culture: Critical Studies of the Thought and Texts of Dante, St. Augustine, St. Thomas Aquinas, Marsilius of Padua, and Other Medieval Subjects.* Firenze: L. S. Olschki, 1964.

Bloch, Ernst. *The Principle of Hope.* 3 vols. Translated by Neville Plaice, Stephen Plaice, and Paul Knight. Cambridge, MA: The MIT Press, 1986.

Booker, M. Keith. *Dystopian Literature: A Theory and Research Guide.* Westport, CT: Greenwood Press, 1994.

————. *The Dystopian Impulse in Modern Literature: Fiction as Social Criticism.* Westport, CT: Greenwood Press, 1994.

Briggs, John C. *Francis Bacon and the Rhetoric of Nature.* Cambridge: Harvard University Press, 1989.

Broad, C. D. *The Philosophy of Francis Bacon.* London: Cambridge University Press, 1926.

Brown, Peter. *Augustine of Hippo: A Biography.* London: Faber & Faber, 1967.

Brown, P. R. L. "Saint Augustine." In *Trends in Medieval Political Thought,* edited by Beryl Smalley, 1-21. Oxford: Basil Blackwell, 1965.

Bruell, Christopher. "On Plato's Political Philosophy." *The Review of Politics* (Spring 1994): 261-82.

Burnell, Peter. "The Problem of Service to Unjust Regimes in Augustine's *City of God.*" *Journal of the History of Ideas* 54 (1993): 177-88.

Bury, J. B. *The Idea of Progress: An Inquiry Into Its Origins and Growth.* New York: Dover Publications, 1955; first published by Macmillan in 1932.

Cachey, Theodore J., Jr., ed. *Dante Now: Current Trends in Dante Studies.* Notre Dame: University of Notre Dame Press, 1995.

Carlyle, A. J. and F. J. C. Hearnshaw. "St. Augustine and *The City of God.*" In *The Social and Political Ideas of Some Great Mediaeval Thinkers,* edited by F. J. C. Hearnshaw, 34-52. New York: Barnes & Noble, Inc., 1928.

Caspari, Fritz. *Humanism and the Social Order in Tudor England.* Chicago: The University of Chicago Press, 1954.

Cassirer, Ernest. *The Platonic Renaissance in England.* Translated by James E. Pettegrove. Austin: University of Texas Press, 1953.

————. *The Individual and the Cosmos in Renaissance Philosophy.* Translated and with an introduction by Mario Domandi. New York: Harper & Row, 1963.

Clarke, I. F. "From Space to Time: The Future is Another Place." *Futures* 7 (September 1990): 752-60.

Cohn, Norman R. *The Pursuit of the Millennium.* Fairlawn, N.J.: Essential Books, 1957.

Collins, Stephen L. *From Divine Cosmos to Sovereign State: An Intellectual History of Consciousness and the Idea of Order in Renaissance England.* New York: Oxford University Press, 1989.

Conze, Edward. "Dharma as a Spiritual, Social, and Cosmic Force." In *The Concept of Order,* edited by Paul G. Kunz, 239-52. Seattle, WA: University of Washington Press, 1968.

Copleston, Frederick. *Ockham to Suarez.* Vol. 3. *A History of Philosophy.* Westminster, MD: Newman Press, 1953.

Cornford, Francis MacDonald. *Plato's Theory of Knowledge.* New York: Humanities Press, 1951.

————, trans. *The Republic of Plato.* New York: Oxford University Press, 1945.

Crowther, J. G. *Francis Bacon: The First Statesman of Science.* London: The Cresset Press, 1960.

Davis, Charles T. "Dante and the Empire." In *The Cambridge Companion to Dante,* edited by Rachael Jacoff, 67-79. New York: Cambridge University Press, 1993.

Dawson, Christopher. *Enquiries into Religion and Culture.* New York: Sheed & Ward, 1937.

————. "Saint Augustine and His Age." In *A Monument to Saint Augustine: Essays on Some Aspects of His Thought,* edited by M. C. D'Arcy, et al, 11-77. London: Sheed and Ward, 1930.

Deane, Herbert A. *The Political and Social Ideas of St. Augustine.* New York: Columbia University Press, 1963.

D'Entréves, A. P., ed. and trans. *Aquinas: Selected Political Writings.* Oxford: Basil Blackwell, 1948.

————. *Dante as a Political Thinker.* London: Oxford University Press, 1952.

————. *The Notion of the State.* London: Oxford University Press, 1967.

Donnelly, Dorothy F. "Reconsidering the Ideal: *The City of God* and Utopian Speculation." In *The City of God: A Collection of Critical Essays,* edited by Dorothy F. Donnelly, 199-211. New York: Peter Lang Publishing, 1995.

————, ed. *The City of God: A Collection of Critical Essays.* New York: Peter Lang Publishing, 1995.

Ehrenberg, Victor. *The Greek State.* New York: Barnes & Noble, 1960.

Elliott, Robert C. *The Shape of Utopia: Studies in a Literary Genre.* Chicago: University of Chicago Press, 1970.

Epictetus. *Discourses.* In *The Stoic and Epicurean Philosophers,* edited by Whitney J. Oates. New York: Random House, 1940.

Epicurus. *Fragments.* In *The Stoic and Epicurean Philosophers,* edited by Whitney J. Oates. New York: Random House, 1940.

Eschmann, I. Th. "Studies on the Notion of Society in St. Thomas Aquinas." *Mediaeval Studies* 8 (1946): 1-42.

Farrington, Benjamin. *The Philosophy of Francis Bacon.* Chicago, IL: University of Chicago Press, 1966.

Faulkner, Robert K. *Francis Bacon and the Project of Progress.* Lanham, MD: Rowman & Littlefield, 1993.

Ferguson, John. *Utopias of the Classical World.* Ithaca, NY: Cornell University Press, 1975.

Figgis, John N. *The Political Aspects of St. Augustine's City of God.* London: Longmans & Green, 1921.

————. *The Divine Right of Kings.* London: Cambridge University Press, 1896. Reprint. New York: Harper & Row, 1965.

Finley, M. I. "Utopianism Ancient and Modern." In *Critical Spirit: Essays in Honor of Herbert Marcuse,* edited by Kurt H. Wolff and Barrington Moore. Boston: Beacon Press, 1967.

Fortin, Ernest L. "St. Thomas Aquinas." In *History of Political Philosophy.* 2nd ed. Edited by Leo Strauss and Joseph Cropsey, 223-50. Chicago: Rand McNally, 1972.

Frankfort, Henri, H. A. Frankfort, John A. Wilson, and Thorkild Jacobsen, eds. *Before Philosophy: The Intellectual Adventure of Ancient Man.* Baltimore: Penguin, 1949.

Freeman, John. "More's Place in 'No Place': The Self-Fashioning Transaction in *Utopia.*" *Texas Studies in Literature and Language* 2 (Summer 1992): 197-217.

Frye, Northrup. "Varieties of Literary Utopias." In *Utopias and Utopian Thought,* edited by Frank E. Manuel, 25-49. Boston: Beacon Press, 1967.

Garin, Eugenio. *Science and Civic Life in the Italian Renaissance.* Translated by Peter Munz. New York: Doubleday, 1969.

Gerber, Richard. *Utopian Fantasy.* London: Routledge & Paul, 1955.

Gewirth, Alan. *The Community of Rights.* Chicago: University of Chicago Press, 1996.

Giamatti, A. Bartlett. *The Earthly Paradise and the Renaissance Epic.* Princeton, NJ: Princeton University Press, 1966.

Gierke, Otto. *Natural Law and the Theory of Society: 1500 to 1800.* Translated and with an introduction by Ernest Barker. Boston: Beacon Press, 1957. (First published by Cambridge University Press in two volumes in 1934.)

Gilson, Etienne. "Dante's Place in History." In *Critical Essays on Dante,* edited by Giuseppe Mazzotta, 119-38. Boston: G. K. Hall, 1991.

Gothoni, Rene and Juha Pentikainen, eds. *Mythology and Cosmic Order.* Helsinki: Suomaiaisen Kirjallisuuden Seura, 1987.

Gunnell, John G. *Political Theory: Tradition and Interpretation.* Cambridge, MA: Winthrop Publishers, Inc., 1979.

Harris, Victor. *All Coherence Gone.* Chicago: University of Chicago Press, 1949.

Hearnshaw, F. J. C., ed. *The Social and Political Ideas of Some Great Mediaeval Thinkers.* New York: Barnes and Noble, 1928.

Hertzler, Joyce O. *The History of Utopian Thought.* New York: Macmillan, 1926.

Hexter, J. H. *More's* Utopia: *The Biography of an Idea.* Princeton, NJ: Princeton University Press, 1952.

Jacoff, Rachel, ed. *The Cambridge Companion to Dante.* New York: Cambridge University Press, 1993.

Jaffa, Harry V. "Aristotle." In *History of Political Philosophy,* 2nd ed. Edited by Leo Strauss and Joseph Cropsey, 64-129. Chicago: Rand McNally, 1972.

Johnson, Harold J., ed. *The Medieval Tradition of Natural Law.* Kalamazoo, MI: Western Michigan University Press, 1987.

Jouvenel, Bertrand de. "Utopia for Practical Purposes." In *Utopias and Utopian Thought,* ed. Frank E. Manual. Boston, MA: Beacon Press, 1967, 219-235.

Kantorowicz, Ernst H. *The King's Two Bodies.* Princeton, NJ: Princeton University Press, 1957.

Kaufman, Peter Iver. "Redeeming Politics: Augustine's Cities of God." In *Redeeming Politics,* ch. 7, 130-48. Princeton, NJ: Princeton University Press, 1990.

Keen, Ralph, and Daniel Kinney, eds. *Thomas More and the Classics.* Angers, France: *Amici Thomae Mori,* 1985.

Kenyon, Timothy. *Utopian Communism and Political Thought in Early Modern England.* London: Pinter Publishers, 1989.

Kolnai, Aurel. *The Utopian Mind and Other Papers: A Critical Study in Moral and Political Philosophy.* Atlantic Highlands, NJ: Athlone Press, 1995.

Kumar, Krishan. *Utopianism.* Minneapolis: University of Minnesota Press, 1991.

Kuntz, Paul G., and Marion Leathers Kuntz. *Jacob's Ladder and the Tree of Life: Concepts of Hierarchy and the Great Chain of Being.* New York: Peter Lang Publishing, 1987.

Kuntz, Paul G., ed. *The Concept of Order.* Seattle, WA: University of Washington Press, 1968.

Lachterman, David R. "The Conquest of Nature and the Ambivalence of Man in the French Enlightenment: Reflections on Condorcet's *Fragment Sur L'Atlantide.*" In *Man, God, and Nature in the Enlightenment,* 37-47. East Lansing, MI: Colleagues Press, 1988.

Lapidge, Michael. "Stoic Cosmology." In *The Stoics,* edited by J. M. Rist, 161-85. Berkeley: University of California Press, 1987.

Leary, John E. *Francis Bacon and the Politics of Science.* Ames: Iowa State University Press, 1994.

Leff, Gordon. *Medieval Thought: St. Augustine to Ockham.* Baltimore: Penguin, 1958.

LeMoine, Fannie, and Christopher Kleinhenz, eds. *Saint Augustine the Bishop: A Book of Essays.* New York: Garland Publishing, 1994.

Levin, Harry. *The Myth of the Golden Age in the Renaissance.* Bloomington: Indiana University Press, 1969.

Levitas, Ruth. *The Concept of Utopia.* Hemel Hempstead, Eng.: Philip Allan, 1990.

Liljegren, S. B. *Studies on the Origin and Early Tradition of English Utopian Fiction.* Copenhagen: Uppsala University Press, 1961.

Logan, George M. *The Meaning of More's Utopia.* Princeton, NJ: Princeton University Press, 1983.

Lovejoy, Arthur O. *The Great Chain of Being: A Study of the History of an Idea.* New York: Harper & Row, 1936.

———, and George Boas. *Primitivism and Related Ideas in Antiquity.* New York: Octagon Books, 1965.

Löwith, Karl. *Meaning in History: The Theological Implications of the Philosophy of History.* Chicago: University of Chicago Press, 1949.

MacKinnon, Patricia L. "Augustine's *City of God:* The Divided Self/The Divided Civitas." In *The City of God: A Collection of Critical Essays,* edited by Dorothy F. Donnelly, 319-52. New York: Peter Lang Publishing, 1995.

McCutcheon, Elizabeth, and Clarence H. Miller, eds. *Utopia Revisited.* Angers, France: *Amici Thomae Mori,* 1994.

McIlwain, Charles H. *The Growth of Political Thought in the West: From the Greeks to the End of the Middle Ages.* New York: Macmillan, 1932.

McMullin, Ernan. "Cosmic Order in Plato and Aristotle." In *The Concept of Order,* edited by Paul G. Kuntz, 63-76. Seattle, WA: University of Washington Press, 1968.

Mancusi-Ungaro, Donna. *Dante and the Empire.* New York: Peter Lang Publishing, 1987.

Mannheim, Karl. *Ideology and Utopia: An Introduction to the Sociology of Knowledge.* Translated by Louis Wirth and Edward Shils. New York: Harcourt Brace, 1940.

Manuel, Frank E., and Fritzie P. Manuel. *Utopian Thought in the Western World.* Cambridge: Harvard University Press, 1979.

Manuel, Frank E., ed. *Utopias and Utopian Thought.* Boston: Beacon Press, 1967.

———. "Toward A Psychological History of Utopias." In *Utopias and Utopian Thought,* 69-98.

Markus, Robert A. *"Saeculum": History and Society in the Theology of St. Augustine.* Cambridge, MA: Cambridge University Press, 1970.

———. "Two Conceptions of Political Authority: Augustine, *De Civitate Dei,* XIX. 14-15, and Some Thirteenth-Century Interpretations." *Journal of Theological Studies* 16 (1965): 68-100.

Marshall, R. T. *Studies in the Political and Socio-Religious Terminology of the De Civitate Dei.* Washington, D.C.: Catholic University Press, 1952.

Marsilius of Padua. *Defensor Pacis.* 2 vols. Translated and with an introduction by Alan Gewirth. New York: Columbia University Press, 1951, 1956. Reprint (2 vols. in 1). New York: Arno Press, 1979.

Mazzotta, Giuseppe. *Critical Essays on Dante.* Boston: G. K. Hall, 1991.

Mell, Donald C., Jr., Theodore E. D. Braun, and Lucia M. Palmer, eds. *Man, God, and Nature in the Enlightenment.* East Lansing, MI: Colleagues Press, 1988.

Mommsen, Theodor E. "St. Augustine and the Christian Idea of Progress: The Background of *The City of God.*" *Journal of the History of Ideas* 12 (1951): 346-74.

More, Thomas. *Utopia.* Vol. 4, *The Complete Works of St. Thomas More,* edited by Edward Surtz, S. J., and J. H. Hexter. New Haven, CT: Yale University Press, 1965.

Mumford, Lewis. *The Story of Utopias.* New York: Viking Press, 1922.

Nederman, Cary J. "Knowledge, Consent and the Critique of Political Representation in Marsiglio of Padua's *Defensor Pacis.*" *Political Studies* 1 (March 1991): 19-35.

———. "Private Will, Public Justice: Household, Community and Consent in Marsiglio of Padua's *Defensor Pacis.*" *Western Political Quarterly* (December 1990): 699-717.

Negley, Glenn, and J. Max Patrick, eds. *The Quest for Utopia: An Anthology of Imaginary Societies.* New York: Henry Schuman, 1952.

Nelson, William, ed. *Twentieth-Century Interpretations of* Utopia. Englewood Cliffs, NJ: Prentice-Hall, 1968.

Nendza, James. "Political Idealism in More's *Utopia.*" *The Review of Politics* (Summer 1984): 428-51.

———. "Religion and Republicanism in More's *Utopia.*" *Western Political Quarterly* (June 1984): 195-211.

Niebuhr, Reinhold. "Augustine's Political Realism." In *The Essential Reinhold Niebuhr: Selected Essays and Addresses,* edited by Robert McAfee Brown, 123-41. New Haven, CT: Yale University Press, 1986.

O'Donovan, Oliver. "Augustine's *City of God* XIX and Western Political Thought." *Dionysius* 11 (1987): 89-110.

Olin, John C., ed. *Interpreting Thomas More's* Utopia. New York: Fordham University Press, 1989.

Oliver, W. Donald. *Theory of Order.* Yellow Springs, OH: The Antioch Press, 1951.

Opanasets, Nicholas. "More Platonism." *The Review of Politics* (Summer 1989): 412-34.

Pagels, Elaine. *Adam, Eve, and the Serpent.* New York: Random House, 1988.

———. "The Politics of Paradise." *Harvard Theological Review* 78 (1985): 67-99.

Parkes, Henry B. *The Divine Order: Western Culture in the Middle Ages and the Renaissance.* New York: Alfred A. Knopf, 1969.

Plato. *Laws.* Translated by A. E. Taylor. In *The Collected Dialogues of Plato,* edited by Edith Hamilton and Hamilton Cairns. New York: Bollingen Foundation, 1961.

———. *Republic.* Translated by Paul Shorey. In *The Collected Dialogues of Plato,* edited by Edith Hamilton and Huntington Cairns. New York: Bollingen Foundation, 1961.

Raitiere, Martin N. "More's *Utopia* and *The City of God.*" *Studies in the Renaissance* XX (1973): 144-68.

Ranasinghe, Nalin. "Deceit, Desire, and the Dialectic: Plato's *Republic* Revisited." *Interpretation: A Journal of Political Philosophy* 3 (Spring 1994): 309-32.

Reeve, C. D. C. "Platonic Politics and the Good." *Political Theory* 23 (August 1995): 411-24.

Reeves, Marjorie. "Marsiglio of Padua and Dante Alighieri." In *Trends in Medieval Political Thought,* edited by Beryl Smalley, 86-105. Oxford: Basil Blackwell, 1965.

Rist, John M. *Stoic Philosophy.* London: Cambridge University Press, 1969.

Rossi, Paolo. *Francis Bacon from Magic to Science.* Translated by Sacha Rabinovitch. Chicago: University of Chicago Press, 1968.

Ruyer, Raymond. *L'utopie et les utopies.* Paris: Presses Universitaires de France, 1950.

Sabine, George H. *A History of Political Theory,* 3rd ed. New York: Holt, Rinehart and Winston, 1961.

Sargent, Lyman Tower. "The Three Faces of Utopianism Revisited." *Utopian Studies* 5 (1994): 1-37.

Sargisson, Lucy. *Contemporary Feminist Utopianism.* New York: Routledge, 1996.

Scully, Edgar. "The Political Limitations of Natural Law in Aquinas." In *The Medieval Tradition of Natural Law,* edited by Harold J. Johnson, 149-159. Kalamazoo, MI: Western Michigan University Press, 1987.

Seth, James. *English Philosophers and Schools of Philosophy.* London: J. M. Dent & Sons, 1912.

Shklar, Judith. "The Political Theory of Utopia: From Melancholy to Nostalgia." In *Utopias and Utopian Thought,* edited by Frank E. Manuel, 101-15. Boston: Beacon Press, 1967.

Smalley, Beryl, ed. *Trends in Medieval Political Thought.* Oxford: Basil Blackwell, 1965.

Smith, Jonathan. *Fact and Feeling: Baconian Science and the Nineteenth-Century Literary Imagination.* Madison: University of Wisconsin Press, 1994.

Stark, Rodney. *The Rise of Christianity: A Sociologist Reconsiders History.* Princeton, NJ: Princeton University Press, 1996.

Starnes, Colin. *The New Republic.* Waterloo, Ont: Wilfrid Laurier University Press, 1990.

Steel, Carlos. "Does Evil Have a Cause? Augustine's Perplexity and Thomas's Answer." *Review of Metaphysics* 2 (December 1994): 251-73.

Strauss, Leo, and Joseph Cropsey, eds. *History of Political Philosophy.* 2nd ed. Chicago: Rand McNally, 1972.

Surtz, S. J. *The Praise of Pleasure: Philosophy, Education, and Communism in More's Utopia.* Cambridge, MA: Harvard University Press, 1957.

———. *The Praise of Wisdom: A Commentary on the Religious and Moral Problems and Backgrounds of St. Thomas More's Utopia.* Chicago: Loyola University Press, 1957.

Suvin, Darko. "Defining the Literary Genre of Utopia: Some Historical Semantics, Some Genealogy, A Proposal and a Plea." *Studies in the Literary Imagination* 6 (Fall 1973): 121-45.

Sweeney, Eileen C. "From Determined Motion to Undetermined Will and Nature to Supernature in Aquinas." *Philosophical Topics* 2 (Fall 1992): 189-214.

Sylvester, Richard S., and Germain P. Marc'hadour, eds. *Essential Articles for the Study of Thomas More.* Hamden, CT.: Archon Books, 1977.

Thompson, Craig R. "The Humanism of More Reappraised." *Thought* 52 (1977): 231-48.

Tillich, Paul. "Critique and Justification of Utopia." In *Utopias and Utopian Thought,* edited by Frank E. Manuel, 296-309. Boston: Beacon Press, 1967.

Tillyard, E. M. W. *The Elizabethan World Picture: A Study of the Idea of Order in the Age of Shakespeare, Donne, and Milton.* New York: Random House, n. d.

Todd, Margo. *Christian Humanism and the Puritan Social Order.* Cambridge, MA: Cambridge University Press, 1987.

Tuveson, Ernest L. *Millennium and Utopia: A Study in the Background of the Idea of Progress.* New York: Harper & Row, 1964.

Ullmann, Walter. *A History of Political Thought: The Middle Ages.* Baltimore, MD: Penguin, 1965.

Verbeke, Gerard. *Stoicism in Medieval Thought.* Washington, D.C.: Catholic University of America Press, 1983.

Vickers, Brian, ed. *Essential Articles for the Study of Francis Bacon.* Hamden, CT: Archon Books, 1968.

———. "Francis Bacon and the Progress of Knowledge." *Journal of the History of Ideas* 3 (1992): 495-518.

Voegelin, Eric. *Order and History.* 4 vols. Baton Rouge: Louisiana State University Press, 1956-1974.

Wallace, Karl R. *Francis Bacon on the Nature of Man.* Urbana: University of Illinois Press, 1967.

Warhaft, Sidney. "The Providential Order in Bacon's New Philosophy." *Studies in the Literary Imagination* 4 (1971): 49-64.

Wegemer, Gerard. *"The City of God* in Thomas More's *Utopia." Renascence* 66 (Winter 1992): 115-35.

Weinberger, Jerry. *Science, Faith, and Politics: Francis Bacon and the Utopian Roots of the Modern Age.* Ithaca, NY: Cornell University Press, 1985.

Weithman, Paul J. "Augustine and Aquinas on Original Sin and the Function of Political Authority." *Journal of the History of Philosophy* 30 (July 1992): 353-76.

White, Howard B. *Peace Among the Willows: The Political Philosophy of Francis Bacon.* The Hague: Martinus Nijhoff, 1968.

White, Thomas I. "Pride and the Public Good: Thomas More's Use of Plato in *Utopia." Journal of the History of Philosophy* 4 (1982): 329-54.

Whitney, Charles. *Francis Bacon and Modernity.* New Haven, CT: Yale University Press, 1986.

Willey, Basil. *The Seventeenth Century Background: Studies in the Thought of the Age in Relation to Poetry and Religion.* New York: Columbia University Press, 1965.

Wolin, Sheldon S. *Politics and Vision: Continuity and Innovation in Western Political Thought.* Boston: Little Brown, 1960.

Index

Index

Index

two orders of membership *see* membership
two realms of being 19, 21, 32, 57, 62
two universal societies concept of 18,
22, 64, 73, 124n33
Ullmann, Walter 34, 73, 110n5
universal society 50, 63-64, 124n33
universal transpolitical society 65, 67
universe as an intelligible whole 62
universe as orderly and rational 88
utopia
and order 12-14, 15, 99
and pastoral 3, 5-6
as openended 6, 12
problem of defining 1-7
descriptive definitions of 1-3
colloquial definitions of 1-2
definitions of that privilege content,
form, or function 12-13
vs. heavenly city 6-7
variety of approaches to understanding and classification of

2-7
demise of classical utopias 15, 99
utopian propensity/utopian impulse 6,
102n11
utopian thought outside the Western
world 102n12
utopianism as discipline-bound 12
Verbeke, Gerard 124n33
Voegelin, Eric 104n30
Wallace, Karl 126n3
Weil, Simone 11
Weinberger, Jerry 131n5
Weithman, Paul 31, 110n1
well-ordered society 48
Wells, H. G. 2
White, Howard 89, 126n3
Whitney, Charles 85, 97, 126n3, 129,
131n5
whole of humanity 47
Wolin, Sheldon 28, 39, 107n15,
109n42, 120n5

About the Author

Dorothy F. Donnelly is Professor of English and currently Chair of the English Department at the University of Rhode Island. She received her doctorate from Brandeis University and a master of arts degree from Brown. In addition to publishing numerous articles in professional journals, she has served as editorial consultant for various publications. She recently edited *The City of God: A Collection of Modern Critical Essays* (1995). Professor Donnelly is a recipient of a Teaching Excellence Award from the University of Rhode Island.

DATE DUE

JUN 3 0 2009			
			Printed in USA